COLLECTING BOOKS IN NEW ENGLAND

An Introduction for the Beginning Collector and the Home Library Builder, With Directories of Used Book Shops and Annual Used Book Sales

CO-AZV-924

L. A. Collins

Production by
Ed Hogan & Ann Marie McKinnon
Aspect Composition
13 Robinson St., Somerville, Mass. 02145

Design by Ed Hogan

Printed by Thomson-Shore, Inc.
Dexter, Michigan

This book was printed on acid-free paper and the binding Smyth sewn to promote book longevity.

ISBN 0-913125-00-8
Library of Congress Catalogue Card No. 83-81117

Robert J. Diefendorf, Publisher
RFD 145
West Lebanon, Maine 04027

Special thanks to the librarians and staff of the
Rochester Public Library, Rochester, New Hampshire

To Booksellers and
Annual Used-Book Sale Sponsors

We sent letters with stamped, self-addressed envelopes to all the booksellers we could locate through directories and regional lists, asking if they would allow us to list them in a guide for new collectors and home library builders.

I have no doubt that we did not reach some booksellers and apologize to those we missed. Please send us information about your shop and you will be included in future editions.

We sent letters to libraries and organizations that sponsor annual book sales, but since some of these sales are not widely advertised, or advertised in special interest publications, there is no permanent source of information about them. We made many telephone calls to insure that as many of these worthy sales as possible would be listed.

If your library or organization used book sale is not listed, and you would like to be in future editions of this book, send us your information.

Table of Contents

Old Books, New Books 7
Collecting Children's Books 13
American Ephemera 21
Comic Books 27
Americana 31
Mystery and Detective Fiction 37
Dealer and Auction House Catalogues........................45
Investing/Collecting 51
Antiquarian Book Fairs 57
The Collector's Reference Shelf 61
Collecting Books for the Home Library........................65
Home Library for Children 73
Used Book Sales 81
Used Book Sales in New England 89
Used Booksellers 127
Used Booksellers in New England 133
Indexes..181

I believe books will never disappear. It is impossible for it to happen. Of all of mankind's diverse tools, undoubtedly the most astonishing are his books . . . . Humanity's vigils have generated infinite pages of infinite books. Mankind owes all that we are to the written word. . . . . Books are the great memory of the centuries. Consequently their function is irreplaceable. If books were to disappear, history would disappear. So would men.

Jorge Luis Borges, in Horizon *magazine*

Old Books, New Books

When we read in the newspaper of Doctor Armand Hammer's purchase, for over five million dollars, of Leonardo DaVinci's handwritten notebook, *Of the Nature, Weight and Movement of Water,* or hear of a book speculator who buys up fifty first editions of every new best-seller, hot off the presses, for "investment," we are confirmed in our belief that old books and first editions are what book collecting is all about. But this is not necessarily so.

The age of a book does not necessarily make it collectible. There are a lot of old books around, collections of old sermons in Greek and Latin, history texts that were printed in the tens of thousands and are of no cultural or historical significance. They said no new thing, nor did they illuminate any old idea or challenge it, as Martin Luther's works did in his time, and Martin Luther King's *Letter from Birmingham Jail* did in our own time.

Works of cultural or historical significance make us see things fresh, and whether or not these works are suppressed or ignored in their own time, they are the precursors of what will be.

Old books that describe new discoveries in science, or the discoveries and explorations of new lands, old books on agriculture, fox hunting, book binding, cooking, fashion, music, art, and many other subjects are considered collectible if they can be collected around a central theme that expands our knowledge of the subject, or they are the first or one of the earliest books printed in a country or region, or are the first to display a new type-face, or come from a famous press, or . . . .

A roomful of old American geographies, collected just because they are old, will be just a roomful of old geographies. But several shelves of old geographies collected around the theme of showing the geographical development

7

of a particular region—say, New England—from its first appearance in geographies as largely wilderness to the formation of its present boundaries, would be a collection with coherence, valuable to researchers, and valuable monetarily as a collection.

First editions of books have value if the author or subject is considered to be of enduring interest. The collecting of "modern firsts" (roughly fiction books from the first part of this century to the present), is popular and sometimes provides an interesting example of the dangers of riding popular bandwagons.

English author Arnold Bennett is rarely read today. His *Clayhanger* and *Hilda Lessways* are still very good novels, and are of interest as social history, but readers do not know of them. Bennett enjoyed enormous popularity in his lifetime. First editions of his novels, signed by him, or unsigned, commanded high prices from dealers and collectors. These same first editions would yield very little on the market today.

At the height of their popular success, authors like Bennett, and John Galsworthy, were eagerly collected. Their popularity and success seemed to guarantee that they would remain sought after. At the same time, during the lowest point of Herman Melville's readership, when few if any of his works were included in American college literature courses, Melville was mentioned in Michael Sadleir's 1922 bibliography of 19th century literature. The following year, one of his books was sold at a British auction house for a few pounds, a pittance compared to the prices then popular authors were getting at auction, authors who enjoyed tremendous popularity in their day but whose names and works are practically forgotten today.

What is of enduring interest is not decided by those who compile best-seller lists. In a recent financial magazine article on the investment possibilities of book collecting, one man told how he no longer invests in the stock market, but puts all his money into books, specifically, modern firsts. He said that he figured that a popular novelist, prominent on best-seller lists, was a "good bet," and bought twenty of this author's latest book, first editions. Presumably he paid the list price, about fifteen dollars for each book. First editions of this particular book began turning up on remainder tables priced $3.98 and under within months of its first issue.

Because of the "hype" surrounding this particular author, his publisher expected enormous sales, so issued a first edition of several hundred thousand. Since scarcity is one factor in determining the price of a collectible book, the book speculator in the magazine article may have to wait a while before his twenty copies of the "good bet" appreciate to the point where he can realize their original cost.

An article, "The Decline of Editing," in *Time* magazine (September 1, 1980) described the changes in publishing since the early part of this century when collectors began collecting modern authors as a separate specialty. "The pressure on the publishing assembly line is increasing. Trendy books on jogging, herbal medicine, and bio-feedback must be out by the cash register, before the next craze sends them to the remainder pile.

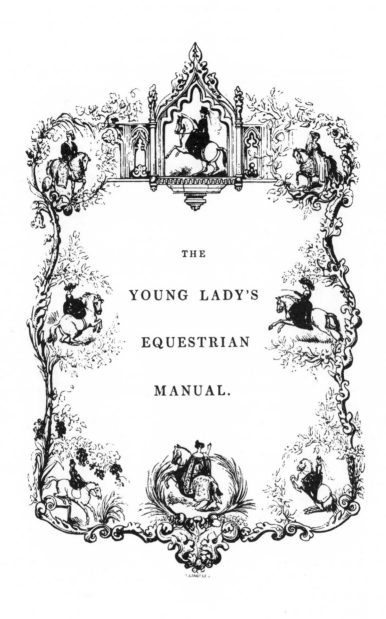

THE

YOUNG LADY'S

EQUESTRIAN

MANUAL.

A title page from a valuable, old book, printed in London, 1838.

"Novels with big advances behind them have to be whizzed through so the publisher can get back his investment. . . . In such a frenzied atmosphere, the word *book* may give way in favor of *project, package, hot property* and *blockbuster.* Even editors of non-commercial novels and belles-lettres feel the pressures to score with a MERV missile, a work that will get its author on a TV talk show."

Publishers who publish real books rely on the same distribution system that the junk publishers use. Since distributors and retail book outlets, except for the independent retail book stores, are primarily interested in the quick kill—get in, get it and get out—the fine first novel of a serious writer, or the translations of important foreign works that need time to be brought to the attention of the serious reader, are pushed off the store shelves to make way for this week's "blockbuster."

There have always been different levels of taste in literature, but because of the mass market distribution system that dominates the book trade and the marriage of publishing to Hollywood and television, only one level of taste may be satisfied; as one editor remarked, "It will be the level of the lowest common denominator."

Publishers of worthwhile books are trapped in a system that discourages taking chances on the future, a future beyond the next quarter's balance-sheet.

Because of this situation, among other reasons, it is the opinion of many antiquarian dealers that the speculator who buys cartons of best-sellers and "hot" authors contributes nothing to the preservation of a literary heritage. The speculator's "collection" is a dubious enterprise at best, since scarcity and demand are determinants in the future monetary evaluation of books, and junk we will always have with us.

Book collecting includes a far wider range than just old books and modern first editions. Collections are being built around books on travel and exploration, natural history, horticulture (particularly those books with colored or engraved illustrations), books on medicine and science, children's books, fine and small press books, genealogies and town histories, books on steamboat travel, the Civil War, books about railroads, and books by and about American writers in Paris in the Twenties, cookbooks, and books on gardening.

The used book booksellers in this guide's directory offer all the above specialties and a great many others.

If you have accumulated books on a particular subject over the years and would like advice and direction on shaping them into a coherent collection, seek a dealer or several dealers, who specialize in your subject. Since collecting is a life-long affair with books, it is necessary to be as careful in choosing a dealer as in choosing a spouse—probably more so.

Although contemporary mores encourage alterations in feelings to accommodate our "changing needs," "new options in relationships," and so on, most rare book dealers and collectors display a devotion to their specialties that is as enduring as it is passionately intense. A spouse or lover may become, over time, boringly familiar, but the subject of a book collection always appears fresh, offering tantalizing possibilities, continuing interest, and bliss unknown to those who collect other things, including "relationships." This may be the reason why few, if any, antiquarian dealers or serious collectors are found wandering in our culture's psychotherapeutic undergrowth.

Though you will be able to add books to your collection from used-book sales and other sources, dealers are in a better position to find books for your collection that are in superior condition, and condition is important in collecting. Dealers are in touch with the market, know which collections are going to auction, which estates containing books in your specialty are for sale, which collectors are willing to sell duplicate copies from their collections.

The following chapters are brief introductions to some book collecting specialties.

Collecting Children's Books

Ten years ago juveniles had a small, but stable place in the world of book collecting. Usually dealers carried a small stock of rare children's classics, but the major purchases in this subject area were by curators and librarians adding to already existing collections, such as the New York Public Library and the J. Pierpont Morgan Library, among others.

In an inflated economy many people invest their money in collectibles—art, metals, oriental rugs, anything that seems likely to appreciate in tune with inflation. In the 1970's the rare book market attracted many such investors. Children's books, particularly those illustrated by famous artists, saw spectacular increases in prices.

Books illustrated by W. W. Denslow, Walter Crane, Howard Pyle, N. C. Wyeth and other fine artists fetched prices not far behind prices for their original works. In some cases, such as books illustrated by Arthur Rackham, the prices paid for just regular trade editions were driven to unrealistic heights by speculators, although many of these books are not scarce.

In the rare book trade if a high price is paid at auction for a book that is still available in fairly large numbers outside the auction room, it does not necessarily follow that the available books will automatically fetch the auction price, or a higher price. The "drop" in prices of Rackham's books from that paid in the auction room is not so much a decrease in their value as a recognition by experienced dealers and collectors that the auction room price may have been unrealistic in the first place.

Book speculators are a nuisance to reputable dealers and serious collectors.

Speculators distort the market and in doing so drive out responsible collectors and frighten the beginning collector of moderate means.

Even people of severely limited means have built creditable, sometimes distinguished collections by focusing on one aspect of a collectible subject, such as early New England primers, or children's readers in the Western Reserve. They did so at a time when these subjects were overlooked by other collectors and were still available in sufficient numbers and at prices they could afford.

It is the steady, unspectacular collector who provides the trade with consistent growth, creating interest in formerly neglected subjects or new subjects.

It is unfortunate that children's books attracted the speculators, for many would-be collectors are drawn first to children's books as the most familiar and least intimidating books to collect.

Most people remember beloved books from childhood; some are fortunate enough to still have them somewhere around the house. Some children's book collectibles are The Windermere Series of *The Arabian Nights* illustrated by Milo Winter; *Robinson Crusoe* with illustrations by Lynd Ward; *Kinut, A Congo Adventure*, written and stunningly illustrated by Elizabeth Enright; *The Boy Allies at Verdun* by Clair W. Hayes; and fairy tales such as Andrew Lang's series, Hans Christian Andersen, and The Brothers Grimm.

How rich we were in our childhood in our books, however straitened our family circumstances. How poor we sometimes feel as adults even when we are drowning in the material evidence of our wealth, wealth for which we may have paid with our childhood dreams.

Paul Hazard, in his wonderful book, *Books, Children, and Men* (Horn Book, Inc.), writes, "'Give us books,' say the children; 'give us wings. You who are powerful and strong, help us escape to the faraway. Build us azure palaces in the midst of enchanted gardens . . . We are willing to learn everything that we are taught at school, but, please, let us keep our dreams.'"

I believe that people who collect children's books do so in order to recapture those dreams if they have lost them; for those people who have held fast to their dreams, their collections are a testament to their constancy.

Collecting children's books is often more challenging than collecting other specialties, for as one writer has said, "Children not only love their books, they love them to pieces."

Children's books, even some of those in famous collections, bear evidence of hard usage—grimy fingerprints, pencilled scrawls, tattered covers, torn pages, colorful jam smears—what Dr. A. S. W. Rosenbach, probably the most respected collector of children's books, called "charming atrocities."

Children's books are descended from the first book made specifically for children to use themselves—the horn book. The horn book was not a book of bound pages, but a paddle-shaped piece of wood with a lesson page, usually the alphabet, numbers, and the Lord's Prayer. A thin piece of horn sealed the page to protect it from soiling.

A Little History of the Horn Book by Beulah Folmsbee, published by Horn

Book, Incorporated, Boston, is a charming and informative treatise on the horn book and another early children's "book," the battledore. Originally published in 1942, *A Little History* . . . contains illustrations of the horn book including one of filigreed silver, and a mounted facsimile of John Newbery's royal battledore.

This lovely little book is still available from the Horn Book, Inc., 31 St. James Street, Boston, MA 02116, for $8.00 plus 63¢ postage. A handmade replica of a colonial horn book is also available for $5.50 plus 52¢ postage.

Horn Book, Incorporated publishes *The Horn Book* magazine, founded by Bertha Mahony Miller in 1924, a bi-monthly review of children's books and related materials. The magazine is an indispensable aid to librarians, teachers, parents and booksellers in choosing the best of current children's literature. The reviews are scrupulously fair and honest, reflecting Horn Book's founder's commitment to excellence in children's literature.

The beginning collector can acquire a sound background on authors and illustrators of children's books by reading back issues of *Horn Book*; current issues would aid in the development of collections of contemporary children's literature.

Horn books and battledores were tools of instruction in reading and figuring; sermons, morality tales and courtesy books purposed to teach youngsters proper spiritual and social conduct.

Courtesy books form interesting collections. Changing social values can be traced from the earliest courtesy books written for children of the upper classes to the late Victorian and Edwardian courtesy books written for more recent arrivals in the upper strata, still a bit shaky from the climb.

Children's books with no purpose but to delight the child were not printed in any great number or with any consistency until the middle of the eighteenth century.

Before that, children appropriated books written for adults such as Cervantes' *Don Quixote*. They read chap books, small pamphlets, reprints of adult stories with crude woodcut prints, some of which might be considered obscene even in our more permissive time; these were hawked in the streets. Cautionary tales continued to be printed with promises of grim retribution for wayward youth.

The best-selling cautionary tale of all time was written in the middle of the nineteenth century in Germany—*Struwwelpeter* (Slovenly Peter) by Dr. Henrich Hoffman-Donner. Youthful miscreants were burned alive or mutilated. For some reason, this nightmarish tale was immensely popular at a time when children's literature had become more humane. The English edition appeared soon after the publication of Andersen's fairy tales.

It may be that Hoffman-Donner wrote *Struwwelpeter* in reaction to the excesses of traditional cautionary tales, and intended it to be more humorous than terrifying. A translation was published in New York in 1849 with the title *Slovenly Peter or Pleasant Stories and Funny Pictures*. Missing from this edition is the parable of thumb-sucking Konrad whose thumbs are cut off by a

Jessie Willcox Smith illustration for Marion Hill's "Within the Ring of
Singing," in *Frank Leslie's Monthly*, August 1903.

deranged tailor.

Children's literature as a distinctive literature written to be enjoyed originated in the shop of London publisher John Newbery in the early 1740's.
Newbery's *A Pretty Pocket Book* . . . was so popular that he and his assistant,
Benjamin Collins, designed and printed more books to please children. Other
printers followed Newbery's lead. Thomas Bewick, printer and illustrator,
issued in 1818 a retold *Fables of Aesop and Others* with over two hundred examples of Bewick's skill.

In America, New York publisher Hugh Gaine copied the Newbery imprints
(no international copyright then); the Newbery abridged *Adventures of
Robinson Crusoe,* and perhaps the most famous Newbery title, *Goody Two
Shoes,* were issued in America by Gaine, and by Isaiah Thomas.

The majority of children's books continued to be printed for children's education and spiritual edification and this continued through the early part of the
20th century, particularly in America, where religious "tract" books extolled
the virtues of a horde of "little Berthas" and "stalwart Neds." School texts
carried illustrations, wood-cut or copper engraved, and ABC books for the beginning reader continued to be printed with illustrations depicting common
objects children could easily identify.

Alphabet, or ABC books more than any other children's books, reflect the
changing world of childhood. The earliest ABC books depicted objects that
children in the next few generations would not easily recognize—quivers,
riding crops, barrows, farm implements and sporting gear that vanished from
sight with the industrialization of Western societies which severed man's con-
nection with nature and the earth.

Throughout the history of printing, artists and calligraphers have expended
their most loving efforts on ABC books, and collectors have built fine collections
centered on alphabet books from around the world. Some very early ABC books
have been reproduced by Dover Publications.

Contemporary artists still see in ABC books a subject that inspires some of
their most thoughtful work. A recent, superb addition to this specialty is Mary
Azarian's *A Farmer's Alphabet,* published in 1981 by David R. Godine. Even
the child whose cerebral cortex may resemble the configuration of a TV test
pattern can be enthralled by Azarian's richly detailed illustrations.

In all cultures that have a written language, the ABC book is the ancient
keystone of literacy. But the golden thread that binds all cultures together, despite barriers of language and custom, is spun out by the tellers of fairy tales.

Readers may not know of the Perraults who, in the 17th century, wrote
stories based on French folk tales, but we all know Cinderella, Sleeping Beauty,
and other fairy tale figures the Perraults gave to the world.

The scholarly collections of German folk tales compiled by Jacob and
Wilhelm Grimm brought Hansel and Gretel, Little Red Riding Hood, Rum-
pelstiltskin, and The Brave Little Tailor to every corner of the globe.

The most beloved of all fairy-tale tellers is Hans Christian Andersen.
Andersen spoke directly to children, to their loneliness, to their steadfastness,

their courage and innocence. Who can forget the tin soldier, so full of love for the porcelain dancer who scorns him, or the little mermaid immortalized in Andersen's story?

Perhaps it is the immortality of these tales that inspires artists in every generation to illustrate them. New, beautifully made editions of old fairy tales continue to be issued and collected. Books like the recently published *The Month Brothers* (Morrow and Company) translated by Thomas P. Whitney and illustrated by Diane Stanley, will be sought after in the future, not only for their stories, but for their illustrations.

Many contemproary children's books have already achieved the status of classics; Roald Dahl, Maurice Sendak, the late Albert Lamorisse, Astrid Lindgren and many other writers from all countries add to the treasury of children's literature.

Collectors may build their collections around a favored artist or author, or on certain themes such as run-aways, orphans, or dolls. Some collectors prefer to take a certain period. The Victorian and Edwardian periods are especially rich in children's books, particularly books illustrated by great artists of that time. An unusual and historically significant theme would be children's books printed in a totalitarian country and those printed in a country with more democratic institutions during the same period.

Very early children's books are scarce and sought after by libraries for their rare book collections, so the competition is keen; but they still do turn up on library tables in rural towns and at used-book sales.

The immense popularity of certain illustrators has caused collectors to turn to less well known illustrators of the same period, although not in the numbers that still want Rackham, Pyle and others. Merely because an artist or author does not figure prominently in dealer and auction house catalogues does not mean that they are not collectible. Catalogues will naturally emphasize that which is being sought after at a particular time, but experienced dealers and collectors are always seeking new areas of a specialty to collect as other areas become crowded, and books in these new areas will be comparatively inexpensive, until they too become popular.

Beginning collectors should consult their own tastes, and in this specialty, as in others, never buy something you don't particularly like merely because it is popular. If you buy something merely because others are clamoring for it and you pay a high price, you will be doubly dissatisfied if it is not something that is of itself pleasurable to you.

Many people will add every children's book that appeals to them to their collections; indeed, some people do not consider their several hundred children's books dating from the mid-eighteenth century to the present a collection at all. Each book is, as one gentleman with about two thousand children's books in his library said, "something I could not resist."

That should be the criterion for collectors in all specialties.

Reference List for Collecting Children's Books

Books and Periodicals

Early Children's Books and Their Illustrators. New York, 1975: The Pierpont Morgan Library. David R. Godine, Publisher (306 Dartmouth St., Boston, MA 02116).

Early American Children's Books. A. S. W. Rosenbach. Dover Publications, Inc. (180 Varick St., New York, NY 10014).

Dover Publications catalogue of children's books.

The Hewins Lectures, 1947-1962, edited by Siri Andrews. Horn Book (Park Square Building, Boston, MA 02116), 1963.

Peter Parley to Penrod: A Bibliographical Description of the Best-Loved American Juvenile Books. Cambridge, Mass., Research Classics, 1961.

Bibliophile in the Nursery, William Targ. Cleveland, The World Publishing Company, 1957.

Forgotten Books of the American Nursery, a history of the development of the American story-book, by Rosalie V. Halsey. Boston, Charles E. Goodspeed, 1911.

Dr. Rosenbach considered Halsey's book to be "the first really good account of the early juvenile literature in America."

A Critical History of Children's Literature, a survey of children's books in English from earliest times to the present, edited by Cornelia Meigs. New York, Macmillan, 1953.

Old Textbooks: Spelling, Grammar, Reading, Arithmetic, Geography, American History, Civil Government, Physiology, Penmanship, Art, Music, as Taught in the Common Schools from Colonial Days to 1900, by John A. Nietz. University of Pittsburgh Press, 1961.

Nietz's book is indispensable for the collector of old school geographies and other school textbooks.

"Children's Books of Long Ago," Wilbur M. Stone. *Saturday Review of Literature,* Vol. 5, March 9 and 23, 1929, pp. 762-763, 810-812; April 6, pp. 864-865. Stone discusses chapbooks, miniatures and early Victorian children's literature.

Wilbur Macey Stone wrote many articles about children's books, including *The History of Little Goody Two-Shoes,* an essay with a list of known editions of this children's classic. It was reprinted from the Proceedings of the American Antiquarian Society for October, 1939, by the American Antiquarian Society, Worcester, Mass.

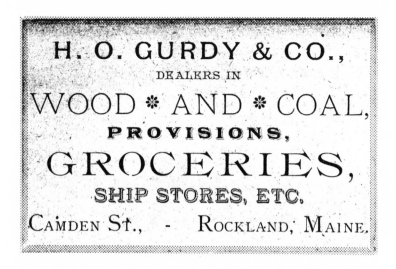

H. O. GURDY & CO.,

DEALERS IN

WOOD ✳ AND ✳ COAL,

PROVISIONS,

GROCERIES,

SHIP STORES, ETC.

CAMDEN St., - ROCKLAND, MAINE.

American Ephemera

"Ephemera," in entymology, is that class of insects, like the May-fly, whose life-span is measured in hours or a day. The word is from the Greek, meaning "lasting but a day." In collecting, the word "ephemera" is applied to usually unbound printed matter issued to be used and discarded. It includes railroad timetables, postcards, menus, trade cards (advertisements for everything from chocolates to motor cars), valentines, posters, political broadsides and pamphlets—whatever would catch attention, relay a message, render a service for a short time, be passed around and thrown away when its usefulness was over.

Probably the most well known of American ephemera are the baseball cards that came with bubble gum. These cards have been collected for generations by baseball fans of all ages. The star players could be traded for lesser lights, one star for several non-stars. The player's picture was on one side of the cards and a brief account of his ballplaying career and game record was printed on the reverse. Early baseball cards are traded now by collectors with as much seriousness as single plays from the Shakespeare folios, and the prices are no laughing matter.

Fortunately for historians and collectors, people save things.

Rare book dealers and collectors have always been interested in ephemera from the earliest days of printing. Antiquarian dealers and collectors of Americana have built major collections around this unbound, printed paper.

Unity

In White Cars the perfect relation of every working part to the other,- the harmonious proportion of all, gives a lasting satisfaction found in no other car. The day is past when a car can long exist because of one or two much extolled features. The beauty and usefulness of White Cars endure, because they are designed and built in the White Factory as a consistent unit.

THE WHITE COMPANY
CLEVELAND

~ Otho Cushing ~

Mercury discards his wingéd sandals for the White Six

From *National Geographic*, May 1914.

The political broadsides and pamphlets of the pre-Revolutionary period in America, detail the struggle of conscience and will engaged in by American colonists to justify or repudiate the idea of separation from the British Crown. These soul-searching exercises went on from the earliest period of our existence as colonial subjects up to the firing of the first shot at the Concord-Lexington Bridge.

The most famous of these pamphlets are those written by Thomas Paine, that almost forgotten, ever contemporary man of genius. His "Common Sense" was a thrilling, dangerous, and ultimately persuasive argument for American independence. But other pamphlet writers were significant in this debate. Their pamphlets were thoughtful, or fiery, or doggedly analytical; in the form of sermons, letters, or essays and treatises on political theory. Through ephemera, the wonder and freshness of the past comes to us with an immediacy not found in history texts. Those who were here before us are not mere abstractions when we hold in our hands their diaries or their cherished keepsakes, valentines, letters.

Such items are called trivia or nostalgia items at flea markets. Picked up cheaply by antique dealers, the items are sold as "paper Americana" to book collectors, or as "decorative prints" by decorators who frame them and sell them to "nostalgia buffs" in the cities.

Old diaries, letters, bills of sale and the like have been the stuff of history, the material with which we reconstruct the past: not the past of the lofty, but that of those who went about the business of building countries, farming the land, inventing, starting industries, and selling the products of those industries.

Eileen Power, in her *Medieval People*, recreated the feudal world of England from manor house records, bills of sale, records of crops planted, forges built, bricks made in the manor kilns, the births, deaths and scandals that were part of that life. It is the common people, the serfs and artisans, who come alive for us in her writing; their owners are only dimly present.

What people wore, what they ate, how they preserved food before freezers and refrigerators, how they furnished their houses, what they read, how they decided who to vote for, what medicines they relied on in illness, how they were buried when the medicines did not work, all this fascinates us and does not appear in the official statistical records, nor, unfortunately, in history texts.

We learn about these things from such items as manufacturers' trade cards, which were advertisements for their products. The cards, after the Civil War, were intricately designed, die cut, and vividly colored. The introduction of steel plates to replace the heavy lithographic stones, made the production of these "chromos" easier and cheaper.

With this new process of chromolithography, businesses could advertise their products in the remotest regions of a still relatively unpopulated country. Immigrant settlers, unfamiliar with the English language, would remember, when they went to town for supplies, the red-cheeked milk maid advertising Horlich's malt that was on the calendar in their kitchen and recognize the name on the package at the store. Many immigrants learned English from these attractive trade items, and from the mail-order catalogues, "wish books" that offered them tangible evidence of the rich promise of their new country.

An elderly woman in South Dakota, daughter of Swedish immigrants, told me how her father had reserved one plot of his farm for Mr. Sears and Mr. Roebuck. Whatever profit was made from that plot went for purchases from the Sears and Roebuck catalogue—a washing machine, a sewing machine, and one year, she recalled with special pride, an ornate, walnut parlor organ with a plush upholstered bench. It still had a place of honor in her parlor.

With the development of towns along completed railroad lines, then the motor car and radio, advertising took new turns and the importance of trade cards diminished, but not to today's collectors.

Trade cards, or trade items, such as store displays, paper fans, calendars, almanacs, whatever could get the advertisers' message to people, are categorized under a variety of specialty headings: by product; or artist (although this is difficult since many did their work anonymously); or subject, e.g., Baker's Cocoa and Quaker Oats under "Foods," McCray Ice Boxes and Grand Rapids furniture under "Housewares." A category such as "Housewares" is further broken down by some collectors into sub-specialties such as kitchen equipment or plumbing supplies.

At the third annual conference of the Ephemera Society of America, "Ephemera USA III," the program recognized the growing fascination with these "fragments of the past" with lectures and exhibits on the history of American ephemera and how to collect it. The conference included an attractive and educational exhibit of the trade cards, labels, business stationery, and premiums used by the 19th century food industry to promote its products.

Trade cards and related advertising items also offer fascinating examples of the change in social attitudes over the years. We think of today's concern for personal safety and home security as a recent phenomenon; that is, until we see the ad display of the Savage Arms Company of Utica, New York for its new ten-round automatic pistol.

A woman's hand holds the pistol; a man's hand in profile next to it, demonstrating how to aim. "Not a fear-frozen throat," the ad proclaims to concerned husbands who apparently travel a lot. "A noise, wide awake—dead of night—all alone. She reaches for her ten-shot Savage. *Now* she is guarded—safe. The burglar hears a calm, confident voice, sees the glistening black barrel pointed as the finger of death. If you don't get her a Savage—someday she will have to appeal to the burglar for mercy. You know what *mercy* from a depraved criminal means. Get a Savage *today*."

Today's advice to the homeowner to conciliate the surprised intruder, engaging him in "meaningful dialogue" as you help him fill his sacks with your valuables, would be as startling to the husbands to whom the Savage ad was addressed, as that ad is to our more modern, not to say effete, sensibilities. I'm not sure in what category the Savage ad would be placed: home furnishings or psychological warfare.

Ephemera Reference List

Barbara Andrews, *A Directory of Postcards, Artists, Publishers and Trademarks.* Little Red Caboose Press, 1975.

Bernard Bailyn, *The Ideological Origins of the American Revolution.* Belknap Press of Harvard University, 1976. Bailyn's Pulitzer Prize winning book is essential reading for a clearer understanding of the American Revolution, as well as an excellent source book for the collector of political pamphlets of the pre-Revolutionary period.

Clarence P. Hornung, Ed., *Handbook of Early Advertising Art: Pictorial Volume.* Dover Publications. "Thousands of specimens from Franklin's time to the 1890's—the cream of early commercial art."

George and Dorothy Miller, *Picture Postcards in the United States, 1893-1918.* Clarkson N. Potter, Inc., 1976.

Maurice Rickard, *This Is Ephemera: Collecting Printed Throwaways.* Stephen Greene Press, 1977.

Rickard founded the International Ephemera Society in London in 1975. The Ephemera Society of America was founded in 1977 by William Frost Mobley, Wilbraham, Massachusetts, and others. Membership is twenty dollars a year. Members receive a well-written and informative quarterly newsletter, a directory of Society members and their specialties, and discounts on books through the Society's book service. Since the collecting of ephemera is relatively new, with few major bibliographies or standard reference works outside of the ephemera dealers' catalogues, membership in the Society would be a boon to the serious beginning and long-time collector. For an additional ten dollars members receive the London Society newsletter, *The Ephemerist.* Inquiries about membership may be sent to Lois Meredith, Vice President, Ephemera Society of America, Preston Street, Hillsboro, New Hampshire, 03244.

From *The Judge*, May 1913.

Comic Books

Comic book collecting was once considered a rather raffish, hole-in-corner affair engaged in by people, mostly male, with reading problems.

Ignored, even by collectors of American popular ephemera, the interest in comic books as collectibles has grown steadily, along with the collecting of early crime and detective paperbacks, outside the mainstream of traditional book collecting.

Today, comic book collecting flourishes, with conventions in almost every large city, newsletters, price-guides, and dealers who are knowledgeable about their wares.

There are sub-specialties in comic book collecting. The science fiction specialties centered on devices that were not then invented—chatty computers, laser beam guns, etc., as part of the story line. Some collectors of traditional science fiction complement their collections with comics.

Many fine graphic designers and artists, like Steve Ditko, started their careers as comic book artists; present day poster artist Frank Frazetta lent his considerable talents to the horror comics of the 1950's.

Comic book collectors display the same agelessness and youthful ebullience as their more traditional book collecting counterparts, and the same ingenuous delight at acquiring a rarity. Sam Galentree, proprietor of Iron Horse Comics in Providence, Rhode Island, has owned over a million comic books, but can barely contain his excitement when telling of the first time he saw a *Superman One* plain. He had bought it in a pile of old comic books dumped onto his counter by a customer. Its condition was only fair, so Mr. Galentree sent it out for repairs. Comic books also have their own expert restorers.

For a comic book collector to acquire *Superman One* in such a casual way is equivalent to a collector of Americana picking up the Bay Psalm Book at a church rummage sale. Mr. Galentree eventually sold *Superman One* to a doctor in the Southwest for several thousand dollars.

The early comic books had recognizable heroes, the cowboys, detectives, the boys "gang" series, Flash Gordon, Tarzan, and the obnoxious Katzenjammer kids, Hans and Fritz. The story line was as familiar as those in old Republic Studio films, with good always triumphing over the not so good. Evil was represented by a mastermind, usually Oriental, out to control the universe, or the nasty cattle rustler with a foreign name and faintly Mediterranean features.

The comic book cowboy, Red Ryder and his underaged, Indian sidekick, Little Beaver, were popular in Europe, particularly in France where the myths of the American West seem to have displaced the Song of Roland in the national imagination.

Comic book heroes were not loners or leaders; the idea of the strong man, the super hero, resolving all human difficulties with a sock in the jaw did not emerge in the comic book, to any significant degree, until World War II. The young reader could distance himself from the adulation of Superman by the citizens of Metropolis because Superman, despite his awesome powers, needed to be the very human Clark Kent. I'm not sure the creators of Superman made a conscious decision to humanize their hero, but it was a sound one.

Children perceive adults as all powerful—at least they used to—and what would this Superman do between crises if he were not regulated by the routines of ordinary humans? For children, the line between hero and bully is unnervingly thin.

Joining the male super-heroes was Wonder Woman. She was beautiful and plucky; flicking her delicate wrists, she deflected machine gun bullets to the amazement of her enemies. You see, she wore these magic metal bracelets and . . . well, let me just say that a lot of little girls went to sleep dreaming of what they would do if they had those bracelets, and those great looking boots. Nancy Drew's little blue roadster paled into insignificance beside boots that let you fly all over the place. In her brief red, white, and blue outfit (pack it in, Nancy, in your grey flannel suits and saddle shoes), Wonder Woman not only fought for democracy, but provided an opportunity for us to see the depths of the enemy's un-American swinishness, as it ogled and leered at our star-spangled heroine.

The war effort of World War II reduced the number of these comic books, making some of them especially scarce. Comic book publishers appealed to their readers' patriotism, urging them to turn in their comics to the paper drives conducted throughout the war. After the war, comic book heroes turned to more mundane matters, foiling bank heists, rescuing whole cities threatened with total destruction (this was before urban renewal) by diabolical madmen.

The horror genre of comic books appeared after World War II, reflecting perhaps our inability to make sense of the horrors revealed at the Nuremburg Trials, and the dilemma of an essentially decent people trying to come to terms with Hiroshima and Nagasaki. Our confrontations with evil within and without would never again be as straightforward, for us or our comic book heroes and heroines. Like the comic book *Teenie Weenies,* we all lived under the mushroom now.

The draughtmanship and color of some of these newer comic books, like *Tales from the Crypt* and *Weird Science Fantasy,* were excellent, particularly Educational Comics, which later became Entertainment Comics. But the pictures portrayed torture and gore and seemed to express an almost voluptuous delight in the suffering of the victims. For many, these comic books represented an unhealthy exploitation of the young reader.

The new genre was drawn in a style and had a story line that, as George Orwell wrote of American pulp magazines, "had been perfected by people who brood endlessly on violence." Although many psychiatrists dismissed these comics as harmless, perhaps even useful, catharsis for youthful violence, psychiatrist Frederick Wertham powerfully criticized such comic books in his book, *Seduction of the Innocent.*

Wertham refuted the catharsis theory by suggesting that in their constant exposure to violence the death camp guards would have become sweeter and gentler as day by day they herded helpless people from box-cars to ovens. Wertham was ridiculed by members of his own profession and vilified by first amendment contortionists, but he did not budge. Horror comic books condoned violence and encouraged sadomasochistic behavior.

Senator Estes Kefauver held Congressional hearings on the "serious threat to young minds" many believed these comic books posed. Comic books were not banned, but the hearings influenced the comic book industry to impose regulations on its members.

The hearings were blamed for the subsequent decline of the comic book industry in the sixties. But the young had already turned away from comic books, for right in their own living rooms was a magic box that, at the flick of a knob, would pour out an endless, uninterrupted flood of trash, a visual feast of violence, corruption and cynicism—with sound.

According to one dealer, comic book collectors are mostly male between the ages of seven and senescence. He laments that more women are not interested in collecting comic books. But except for Wonder Woman and Sheena the Jungle Person, comic books do not offer women of any age a very appealing picture of themselves.

If all the comic book women who were chained up to await the malevolent designs of their captors could have shouted "Shazam," turning themselves into powerful caped avengers capable of giving those pests a taste of their own medicine, women might be as enthralled as men with the "Sock, blam, aargh, splat" genre of pop art and writing as seen in the old comic books.

Americana

Americana refers to books and related material about the United States printed in the United States or, if not, having significance to the development of United States culture and history, though not written as history.

The *Bay Psalm Book*, printed by Peter Dyer in 1640, is an important example of Americana. The *Bay Psalm Book* was not finely printed or beautifully bound. It was merely a serviceable aid for divine worship. But, to Americans, and collectors of Americana, the few copies that have come down to us excite an admiration and respect akin to awe, since it is the oldest known book to be printed in North America.

What has been called "the crowning piece of Americana" is not a book, but a letter, now in possession of the New York Public Library. It is the letter written by Christopher Columbus to his friend, Luis de Santangel, in which the explorer relates "the glorious success that our Lord has given me in my voyage." This is considered the first mention in print of Columbus's discovery of America.

Columbus's letter is also an example of the problem some writers on collecting have in defining "Americana." The term "Americana" refers to the United States of America; however, "The Americas" historically meant Central and South America, as well as Mexico and Canada.

There are sub-specialties in Americana, e.g., Western and Southwestern

Americana, Plains, North-Central tier, and Northwestern Americana.

American fiction is not usually considered Americana, although certain fiction, because it elevates the American landscape, events and customs to classic status, might be considered Americana. *The Great Gatsby* might not be considered Americana, though *Huckleberry Finn* is. *Uncle Tom's Cabin* has been categorized as Americana, though *Gone With the Wind* has not. Books, newspapers, and public notices printed in newly opened regions of the United States would be considered Americana, whatever their subjects.

Itinerant printers followed the settlers west, setting up their presses in the new settlements, starting newspapers, publishing legal notices, printing books, and then moving on to newer settlements. The itinerant nature of early printers and a lack of appreciation for the value of American vs. English or European culture, made the collecting and collating of early American printing west of the Alleghenies a formidable undertaking.

An early standard text on American printers and printing was Isaiah Thomas's *History of Printing in America*. Isaiah Thomas also founded the American Antiquarian Society in Worcester, Massachusetts, which still makes its splendid collections of Americana available to the public for study. However, state libraries and state historical societies would undoubtedly be a richer resource for those interested in researching the history of print in their region.

In California, the earliest known book printed in English was printed in San Francisco. The book is entitled *Laws for the Better Government of California During the Military Occupation of the Country by the Forces of the United States*. A very rare piece of Americana, only one copy of it is known to exist.

The United States is so vast that it would be folly to think one could collect everything about every region and period. The important collections are usually focused on a particular state or region or even a county or town. Books, maps, prints, census reports, vital statistics, notable events, establishment of schools, colleges, libraries, manufacturing, newspapers of an area, are the materials out of which all significant collections are made. A small, dusty town in Texas located on the cattle trail to Kansas might seem insignificant, but its history is of immense importance when linked with the histories of other Texas towns in shaping our understanding of Texas and the Southwest.

The famous Thomas W. Streeter collection, now at Yale, is an example of collecting in a particular area and period. Streeter chose Texas between the years 1795 and 1845 and spent thirty years forming one of the most important collections of Americana ever assembled.

William Reese, dealer and authority on Western Americana, in his tribute to Archibald Hanna, Curator of Western Americana at Yale (*AB Bookman*, October 12, 1981), discusses the formation of Yale's unparalleled collection from the direct contributions of private collectors to the interest and help of dealers from all parts of the country. Mr. Reese wrote, "[Mr. Hanna] visited a vast number of dealers both east and west of the Mississippi. Over the years it was this group who built the solid underpinnings of a reference collection for

Yale, providing scarce and ephemeral local history and odd promotional pamphlets as well as notable high spots."

It is to the collector's advantage to have the assistance of dealers who are knowledgeable in his or her specialty. In few specialties is this more important than Americana. Dealers usually carry the specialties that are of particular interest to them, and if the specialty is their own local history, dealers can assist the collector in focusing his collection and finding "the ephemeral local history and the odd promotional pamphlet."

We are indebted to those collectors who conceived of a central theme to their collecting and, indifferent to fashion or personal profit, spent much of their lives in realizing it. We can see the evidence of such singular dedication in our many college and university collections, collections belonging to local and state historical societies, and those collections in our public libraries.

The older regions, such as New England and the Southern States, collected longer, so there is more reference material on these regions, including fairly thorough bibliographies. Western and Southwestern Americana has been widely collected by libraries in those regions and by private collectors, but its general popularity as a collecting specialty has grown only within the past twenty years.

Twenty years ago, I met a young high school history teacher in South Dakota at his town's dump. We had seen each other at the auction of a local farm but had not been introduced. The young heirs who had sold the farm had disposed of the leftovers by hauling them to the dump. So, over cartons of books, handwritten diaries, old letters and photographs, gilt and flowered candy boxes stuffed with post cards, valentines, old trade cards, we introduced ourselves and set to sorting and deciding what each of us would take. He collected diaries, photographs, early newspapers, letters and town reports and used his materials in his high school classes. I had not been long in that area but had been struck by the almost universal lack of interest of local people in their history.

My new friend told me that many of these towns had been settled by Scandinavians, Bohemians, and Germans. Most had been farmers and a sod-house in the family background was not unknown to them. He had asked several of the older residents to come into his classes and discuss what it had been like to come into a strange country, to make new lives for themselves. Everyone he had asked refused. It had been hard, he learned gradually; some of the women had gone into service as domestics in the households in town; there was embarrassment and some mistrust. Why should they go and tell their neighbors' children they had lived in sod houses? They had big houses now, big farms; they drove big cars and went to Arizona and California in the winter. Why bring up all those bad memories? Their children and grandchildren had been educated and went to work as engineers, accountants, doctors, lawyers, and businessmen in the Twin Cities or Chicago, Omaha and some even to California. The farms the old people had worked, and that had paid for the educations that had scattered their children, would soon pass into other hands.

N.C. Wyeth illustration from August, 1903 Frank Leslie's
Popular Monthly.

The young teacher said he could trace no regret in the old people that their children would not come back and work the farm. One woman had said, "That's what it was all for. So they could have a better life." But he continued to pick up what was cast away as unimportant, realizing that it was the material of history, not as grand or imposing a history perhaps as that of the countries from which his neighbors had come, but none-the-less as stirring.

He told me that I was the first person who had ever bid for the same things he bid on at an auction, books and old periodicals. But he was not displeased. He said he was reassured by the interest of an outsider. He was tenacious of his vision and was not discouraged by the indifference of his neighbors, nor by the lack of interest displayed by the one book dealer he had access to, in a city in the next state. The dealer specialized in first editions and although uninterested himself in local history, the dealer did pick up material at auctions, usually for nothing after auctions, since few bidders were interested in cartons of old papers, maps and books, and he kept an eye open for material the school teacher might want.

It seems incredible to me now that we two standing on a mound in that dump (the highest spot on that particular prairie) were able to salvage early town maps, many hand drawn; a handwritten transcript of the only murder trial in that county; handwritten diaries, one starting out in Danish on ship-board when the settler embarked for America and gradually introducing English words and phrases; a rough draft of the first state constitution; many old children's books in English and Danish, including an early Danish edition of Hans Christian Andersen's fairy tales.

Collecting Plains State material is growing and I doubt that very much of this material is hauled away to dumps today. Bibliographies are being written, but as yet they are not nearly as complete as the known material would call for. This is also true for the Northwestern section of the country, although dealers and collectors in these areas are rigorously pursuing and preserving their share of Americana.

Evaluating what is worth collecting in the absence of a standard bibliography, or of authorities becomes, of necessity, a quite personal approach.

A young dancer touring with a regional theater road company was impressed that in many of the Rocky Mountain towns in which the company appeared an older resident, after the show, would reminisce to the girl about the lovely opera house that used to be in town and the wonderful performances she had seen there. Since the company usually performed in the auditorium of the consolidated high school, the idea that the town had had a house in which theater troupes appeared regularly inspired the young dancer to trace the history of these theaters, their architecture, the people who capitalized and ran them, and the plays and musical performances that had been done in them.

She contacted state libraries, colleges, and regional and local newspapers. She began visiting newspapers in the towns. Since newspapers in small towns still do commercial printing, she thought she might acquire old playbills and newspaper articles on the old opera houses. She is still pursuing this interest, which is providing a colorful addition to that area's history.

Americans move about the country, settling in one place, pulling up stakes and moving to another, and if they value their books and memorabilia, they do find room for them. Books about the West and the Western expansion are not plentiful at used book sales in New England but they do turn up, as do histories of New England towns in Seattle or Houston. But generally speaking, the area in which you live will offer more opportunities for developing a specialty related to that area.

The collections being formed today will be added to our store of knowledge about who we are and where we come from. These collections will enrich the lives of those who come after us.

Americana Reference List

Blanck, Jacob. *Bibliography of American Literature.* Yale University Press, 1955-1973.

Howes, Wright. *U.S. Iana (1650-1950), A Selective Bibliography.* New York, 1962. Revised and enlarged edition.

Thomas, Isaiah. *The History of Printing in America.*

Mystery and Detective Fiction

In the introduction to his *The Further Rivals of Sherlock Holmes* (Pantheon Books, 1973), Sir Hugh Greene discusses the relative abundance and inexpensiveness of 19th and early 20th century mystery and detective material when he first began his "Rivals" series in the 1950's.

"During that decade prices remained fairly steady—apart from a few much-collected authors like Conan Doyle. During the last twelve years prices have multiplied by ten, twenty, even by a hundred times." Although mystery and detective fiction has always had a loyal following of collectors, its increasing popularity as a specialty is a relatively recent phenomenon.

As with all specialties, collectors of mystery and detective fiction may focus on one aspect. Murder might be broken down into sub-specialties such as methods or motives. Many collectors disdain murderers, considering them, as mystery writer His Honour Matthias McDonnell Bodkin, Q.C., did, "the most stupid criminals." His Honour considered confidence men the "best material."

Although detective fiction is considered by many to be a distinctively British literary form, American Edgar Allan Poe appears to have been the first in the field with the publication in the April, 1841 *Gentleman's Magazine* of "Murders in the Rue Morgue." Although popular in his time, both in America and abroad, Poe's amateur detective, Monsieur C. Auguste Dupin, did not acquire the loyal following of that other gifted amateur who appeared about fifty years later.

Dupin solved his mysteries in a "frigid and analytical manner," according to Poe, who ascribed Dupin's detecting abilities not to an informed intelligence exhibiting deductive powers based on logic, but to an "excited, or perhaps diseased intelligence." We know little of Dupin's private life, his personal quirks and eccentricities. Poe was too much involved with Dupin as himself to observe and lovingly relate such things, so Dupin remains a fugitive figure of Poe's own excitable imagination.

Not so with Sherlock Holmes. Sir Arthur Conan Doyle, nearly fifty years after Dupin's appearance, was satisfied to approach his creation as a friend and valued assistant in the character of Doctor Watson. Watson rounds Holmes out for us. Through the good doctor's eyes we see Holmes not as a formidable logic machine, but as a man like the rest of us, who is curious and reflective. Holmes was a private man, but eminently clubbable, as Dupin was not. Between Dupin and Holmes there were other detectives, and Miss Marple was not the first woman to apply her intellect to solving mysteries.

Perhaps the most successful detective story of the Victorian period was Fergus Hume's *The Mystery of a Hansom Cab,* which sold several hundred thousand copies but earned for its author not much more than the fifty pounds for which he sold the copyright. Although Hume continued to write throughout his life, none of his books achieved the success of the first. *The Mystery of a Hansom Cab* is again available through Dover Publications' excellent reprint collection of mystery and detective fiction.

Though the detective story may have originated in America (interestingly, Poe chose Paris for a setting, and a Frenchman for his detective), the golden age of the detective story occurred in Britain in the Victorian and Edwardian periods. Wilkie Collins's first mystery, *Hide and Seek,* was published in 1854; his later *The Moonstone* and *Woman in White* are still read today.

What attracts readers and collectors to the English detective story of the Victorian and Edwardian style is not just the literate quality of the writing and the picture of a materially and socially well-ordered world (if only for a privileged few), but the existence of an established moral code. It was a world where standards of conduct, of what is and is not acceptable in a civilized society, were firmly in place and appeared to be unassailable. One could commit a murder, or several murders, for greed, envy, fear, or for any of the other commonplace spurs that prick our vanity and drive our ambitions, and still be afforded a certain amount of sympathy.

But generally one could not brutalize one's victims. The graphic depictions of torture and mayhem, of deliberate cruelty and sadism present in contemporary murders, in fiction and in fact, would have been offensive to all classes. Instead of keeping our sympathy, through the recognition of a shared human frailty, the murderer would be judged a "nasty brute."

Attacks on the weak and powerless were not tolerated. Servants and old nannies were relatively safe no matter how many corpses turned up in the breakfast room. Servants rarely had the diamond necklaces the murderer wanted, nor were they apt to be claimants in a will, or to be asked to stand for the Commons at the next election, so were considered neglible victims. Class distinctions appear to have been as scrupulously maintained in the morgue as in the drawing room. Nannies and butlers who did seek to improve their financial position by blackmailing their employers could be disposed of without qualm. Betrayal of a trust was recognized as "not cricket" and anyway servants were plentiful.

Victorian and Edwardian detectives did not usually engage in dalliances with their clients, nor with anyone else. And if they did, they did so in private. Only a cad or a wanton would bore others with detailed descriptions. Panting occurred, but only as a consequence of an injudicious chase across a moor too soon after a nine-course meal, with assorted wines, at the grange house.

The code of murderer and sleuth reflected the code of the society at large. And that code was not merely a set of arbitrary rules established to keep the lower classes down while providing rituals by which members of the upper classes could recognize one another. The middle and lower classes continued to cling to this code, recognizing that decency, fair play, compassion, courage and loyalty were vital to the preservation of a workable society, long after the leaders of society had abandoned these principles as "unrealistic."

The real world for these realists was that adumbrated by Freud, Marx and Nietzche. The "nasty brute" became an object of admiration, a man who knew what he wanted and kicked and bludgeoned with relish anyone who got in his way. The degenerate, the boor, the thug were exalted; supposedly, they translated our own darkest fantasies into "healthy" action. The superman, the loner, the outsider, the tough guy became the hero-criminal and the anti-hero detectives as well.

In America, Dashiell Hammett was the earliest exponent of this "hard-boiled" school of detective fiction; later, writers such as Raymond Chandler and James M. Cain created their versions of the existential anti-hero long before Sartre and Camus did, and they placed him in a landscape unremittingly coarse and banal.

The code of the "hard-boiled" detective is shared by the criminal: it is brief and to the point—might is right. Brains are for splattering on pavements; the fist, the jackboot and the gun are modern man's tools for survival. It is interesting to note that at the same time the "hard-boiled" realists of detective, and even "serious" fiction were growing in popularity, the thug as hero was dominating European politics. The abstractions of power and will that provided amusement for a generation of artists and intellectuals became the grim reality of torture, forced labor, and final solutions for millions of people.

George Orwell in his essay, "Raffles and Miss Blandish" (*As I Please, 1943-45*, Harcourt Brace Jovanovich, 1968), wrote, "the growth of 'realism' has been the great feature of the intellectual history of our own age. The interconnection between sadism, masochism, success worship, power worship, nationalism and totalitarianism is a huge subject whose edges have barely been scratched, and even to mention it is considered somewhat indelicate. . . . It is important to notice that the cult of power tends to be mixed up with a love of cruelty and wickedness *for their own sakes*."

This "cult of power" or "bully worship" is the motive force in much of the hard-boiled detective fiction, and in our so-called "serious" fiction. Some writers cannot seem to get enough of it and, not content with spinning out their fascistic daydreams of being the toughest, nastiest little beast on the block, they have taken to haunting death row hoping to immortalize the ultimate bullies in frankly admiring prose.

Our attitudes towards murderers appear to have changed profoundly since the appearance of Dick Donovan's *The Problem of Dead Wood Hall*. Although there is no doubt in the reader's mind that Job Parton, out of jealousy, has killed two men by poison, the jury cannot convict on the evidence presented. "And so Job Parton went free," Donovan writes, "but an evil odour seemed to cling about him; he was shunned by his former companions, and many a suspicious glance was directed to him, and many a bated murmur was uttered as he passed by, until in a while he went forth beyond the seas, to the far wild west . . . ."

Today Job Parton would be met at the "wild west" airport by representatives of television stations and newspapers; publishers would fall all over themselves for the rights to his life story, and the *Job Parton Cookbook* would be on the best seller list the next week. Job would be fawned over on television talk shows and invited on the lecture circuit at handsome fees.

Our confusion about what to do about those who rend the social fabric out of "a love of cruelty and wickedness *for their own sakes*" is compounded by the artists and intellectuals who romanticize what is pathological in society. Champions of the hard-boiled school of "realism" sometimes sneer at more restrained detective fiction, referring to it as "the poisoned bon-bon" school; the reflective, civilized detective who refrains from pistol-whipping a recalcitrant witness is a "cream-puff," a "softie," or worse, an "amateur."

A great many of the golden age's detectives were amateurs who wore many other hats. They were Oxford scholars, artists, former military men with decorations for uncommon bravery; they were journalists, sportsmen, scientists, magistrates, members of Her Majesty's Secret Service, or country schoolteachers. They were, and continue to be, far more realistic and interesting than the narrowly defined hard-boiled detective.

The outsider, the loner, whether criminal or detective, is a truly dreary person. When not beating up someone (and hard-boiled writers take an almost voluptuous delight in describing these scenes) the tough-guy exists in a limbo of physical and intellectual inaction. He has no interests, no allegiances, no affections. He seems to come alive only when he is bashing someone around, or being bashed around. Even his sexual encounters, however violent, reveal a crippling impotence.

The hard-boiled detective does not seem to live anywhere outside of his seedy office or late model automobile. He has no books or flowers or music about him. The quintessential toughie drinks a lot of bad whiskey—straight, no "cream-puff" wines or soda water for him. And he is what his golden age counterparts never are: almost moronically incurious, except, perhaps, about how someone's face would feel being ground to a pulp by the toughie's fists. So unspeakably monotonous are the lives of hard-boiled detectives that they welcome almost any interruption.

Not so with the amateurs, who at times resented any intrusions into their lives. There was so much in the world from which to gain pleasure, so much to learn, so many puzzles to figure out, that even the arrival of a rich, potential client could be a nuisance.

For the amateur (and professional) detective of the golden age, detecting was merely another facet of their multi-faceted lives. They brought to their detective work the knowledge of their own professions—medicine, journalism, the law. They also brought an understanding of humanity based on their involvement with humanity that the loner, the tough guy, does not have.

Realism, if it were truly realistic, would not be just about cruelty and the perverse, which is marginal to most people's lives. True realism would show the connectedness of social orders which makes crimes against that order a matter of concern for all of its members.

Dick Francis writes (and how he writes!) about the world of the race course, its jockeys, trainers, owners, bookmakers, bettors. There are regulations and rules: certain things are not done. Owners are not permitted to lie about the time of a foaling, for that would alter the categorizing of horses by age in a race. Trainers are discouraged from drugging their or others' horses—bad form, as well as illegal. Dick Francis's world might appear raffish to some people, but it is a world with a code, acknowledged even by those who violate the code.

John LeCarre's novels, descendants of the books of the greatest spy novelist, E. Phillips Oppenheim, contain a world of moral squalor as unappetizing as that in the hard-boiled school, but within this world LeCarre's people accept and act upon a code that connects them in a recognizable order. Smiley may be a lonely man, but he is not a loner. He is an aging spy; his loyalties are to his people, and to a code of moral conduct from which, as Orwell says, "the intellectuals have fled." But even the most jaded cynic cannot resist Smiley's integrity at the end when he confronts the vain and supercilious betrayer of that code.

In concluding "Raffles and Miss Blandish," Orwell considers the social implications of the "hard-boiled" school of realistic detective fiction. "There are no gentlemen and no taboos. Emancipation is complete; Freud and Machiavelli have reached the outer suburbs. Comparing the schoolboy atmosphere of the one book (*Raffles*) with the cruelty and corruption of the other (*No Orchids for Miss Blandish*), one is driven to feel that snobbishness, like hypocrisy, is a check upon behavior whose value from a social point of view has been underrated."

Mystery and detective fiction arose from a Western tradition of communal law and a recognition that no single person could be a law unto himself, that even kings and presidents must bow to the laws that governed all citizens. Today, detective fiction is being written and read in almost every country—even in countries that have not had a long tradition of this concept of law and individual rights.

How this literary form bears up in Africa, Russia, Poland, Japan, India, and other countries that have adapted it, is discussed by Michele Slung in her engaging report on the 1981 Crime Writers International Congress printed in an *AB Bookman's Weekly* special crime literature issue, May 3, 1982.

Though critics and some dealers and collectors still consider mystery and detective fiction not worth their attention, the devotion of readers and collectors alike insures its continued growth as a distinctive and rewarding literary form and collecting specialty.

Mystery and Detective Fiction Reference List

Barzun, Jacques and Taylor, Wendell H. *A Catalog of Crime*. Harper & Row, 1974.

Breen, Jon L. *What About Murder? A Guide to Books About Mystery and Detective Fiction*. Scarecrow Press, Inc. (P.O. Box 656, Metuchen, NJ 08840). A handy guide to books and other reference material on this subject.

Greene, Sir Hugh. *More Rivals . . ., Further Rivals . . .* Pantheon Books, New York, 1973. The author and editor of this series has brought together forgotten works of writers of the golden age of detective fiction, with biographical information and commentary.

Mystery and Detective Fiction from Dover. Dover Publications, Inc. (180 Varick Street, New York, NY 10014). This illustrated list of reprints for sale includes the long out-of-print *Riddle of the Sands* by Erskine Childers.

Tracy, Jack. *The Encyclopedia Sherlockiana*. Avon Books. Illustrated and with maps of Sherlock Holmes's London. Alphabetically arranged descriptions of everything relating to the life and times of Sherlock Holmes and Doctor Watson. Tracy's book is not only indispensable for Sherlockians, it is invaluable as a guide to the physical and cultural world of the Victorians and Edwardians.

Winks, Robin W. *Modus Operandi: An Excursion into Detective Fiction*. David R. Godine Publisher (306 Dartmouth Street, Boston, MA 02116). *Modus* comes with an index so the reader can easily locate any of the number of authors and titles, famous and obscure, mentioned in the text. Winks's essay is not an apologia for this type of fiction, but a thorough discussion of it. Winks is informative, literate, scholarly and entertaining.

Dealer and
Auction House Catalogues

All auction houses issue catalogues for their auctions of rare books and some booksellers issue catalogues listing books they are offering for sale. There is a charge for these catalogues, the price depending on the size, or, in the case of important collections, to support the bibliographical work involved and for illustrations.

Some booksellers do not charge even for well made catalogues, assuming that customers receiving the catalogues will buy from them in sufficient numbers to cover the cost. Usually if recipients of free catalogues do not purchase a certain number of books from the catalogues they are dropped from the mailing list.

Except for mail order booksellers who have indicated they wish to have it known that they issue catalogues, I have not listed dealer catalogues.

If readers are interested in specialties offered by booksellers located at a distance, they may write to those booksellers asking if they issue catalogues and at what price, if any. Always enclose a stamped, self-addressed envelope when making inquiries.

I think that all dealers should charge for their catalogues, although libraries and long-time customers who buy heavily from the catalogues could be excepted. My reason is this: Even catalogues that are simply mimeographed sheets of paper, if they are not wildly inaccurate, are excellent learning tools for the beginner and valuable additions to the collector's reference library.

By checking the information about the same book in several catalogues, collectors can learn what price is "preposterous, what is appropriate, what is sensible, and what is fair. Aided by this knowledge, he will soon be able even to sense what is a bargain." (Peter B. Howard, "American Fiction Since 1960," in *Collectible Books: Some Paths,* ed. Jean Peters, New York, Bowker, 1979).

More importantly, the collector is able, through catalogues, to become familiar with the wide range of books that make up a particular specialty. For the collector of moderate means, most catalogues offer sound titles in subjects that are of interest to the collector for as low as ten dollars or less. The cheapest, most shoddily made paperback "blockbuster" written in a couple of weeks to capitalize on a "movie tie-in," can cost as much as a sturdily bound little volume of Charles Lamb's essays designed and printed by a small, private press in England. Can you imagine turning to that cheap "blockbuster" in future years for sustenance or amusement?

What thoughtfulness or reflection or quiet truths that explode in our minds can be found in these "blockbusters"? They are not the products of a man or woman's solitary struggle to bring order out of dark chaos, and to shape ideas into words with a suppleness and clarity that make us exclaim, "Yes, that is how it is; that is gladness; that is sorrow."

Sometimes when a writer speaks to us, it is not so much what he says on the printed page, but what his words have conjured up that is not stated that pierces our souls.

Dmitri Panin's *The Notebooks of Sologdin* (New York, Harcourt, Brace, Jovanovich, 1973) brims over with this sense of experiencing deeply what is not stated. In one instance, Panin and Solzhenitsyn are together on a transport train to another labor camp on the Gulag. The train stops at a crossroads for a few minutes and the two men casually notice a middle-aged woman standing at the crossing gate. "She was wearing broken, worn-down boots. Her dark clothing was shabby and patched all over." Suddenly both men are startled into attention.

> Large tears were streaming from the woman's eyes. Having made out our silhouettes inside the detention car, she lifted a small, work calloused hand and blessed us with the sign of the cross, again and again. Her diminutive face was wet with tears. We kept staring at her; we simply could not tear our eyes away.

You do not find such affirmations in "blockbusters." The noise of the hype drowns out the quiet announcements of such books as Panin's when they do appear. Fortunately used book shops and booksellers' catalogues preserve them from oblivion.

Dealer and auction catalogues are very important reference sources. Indeed, many of these catalogues are sought years after they are issued. W. E. Morrill's, in Boston, issued a catalogue of children's books several decades ago that is sought after today in the "want" pages of *AB Weekly* by dealers and collectors of children's books. Morrill's no longer carries an extensive collection of children's books, nor is it currently issuing that catalogue, but the early Morrill children's catalogue is still considered a sound reference source.

Many dealer and auction house catalogues increase in value as do the books they list, particularly catalogues of significant collections, or those written by dealer/experts who wrote catalogues on a specialty that was not crowded at the time of the writing.

In 1941, rare book dealer Walter Schatzki issued a catalogue on old and rare children's books. About 1500 copies were sent to dealers and customers, but so authoritative were Mr. Schatzki's listings that the catalogue continued to be sought long after it was out of print. Gale Research Company reprinted the Schatzki catalogue, *Children's Books, Old and Rare*, in 1974. Gale Research books can be ordered by phone, toll free (1-800-521-0707), or by mail to: Gale Research Co., Book Tower, Detroit, MI 48226.

Books are usually listed in catalogues with the author's name first, then title, place where published, date published, and name of publisher. A description of the book follows with reference citations and condition.

If the importance of the book listed lies in its illustrations, the name of the illustrator usually comes first.

The following example of a listing is taken from Skip Brack's *Moosabec Reach Historical Co. Catalogue Number One:*

> UPHAM, Charles Wentworth - LIFE, EXPLORATIONS AND PUBLIC SERVICES OF JOHN CHARLES FREMONT. Boston, 1856. Ticknor and Fields, 12 mo. blind stamped green cloth. 356 p. plus adv.; 9 ills. plus frontis. 1st edition. Excellent: cover sl. spotted; frontis foxed; t.p. v. sl. foxed; text clean, tight and fine. Not listed in Howes; other Upham titles listed. Price $25.00

The size or format of a book is sometimes given in traditional terminology based on the folding of the printed sheet into what becomes in the process of binding, a section of pages. Some booksellers avoid this traditional format listing, stating book size in inches. The Moosabec Reach catalogue prints a brief explanation of format size of the book. A more detailed explanation of book size can be found in Carter's *ABC for Book Collectors,* under "format." "Blind stamp" means that a decoration has been impressed on the cover without coloring or gilt added.

"Green cloth" refers to the binding material and its color.

"356 p. plus adv." means that in addition to the 356 pages that make up the book there are pages advertising books by the same author or other authors' works issued by the same publisher.

For "9 ills. plus frontis," read "9 illustrations plus frontispiece." Frontispiece is usually the first illustration in the book facing the title page.

"First edition." Carter in *ABC for Book Collectors* writes, "This apparently simple term is not always as simple as it appears. The question *when is a first edition not a first edition?* is a favorite debating exercise among bibliographers and advanced collectors."

Since this book is for beginning collectors, "first edition" can be loosely defined as the first appearance of a bound book. And that is loose!

"Excellent" refers to condition. Brack explains the descriptions he uses for condition and "excellent" here means "very slightly worn, or with a defect as described."

"Cover sl. spotted" means that the cover is slightly spotted. Some catalogues describe spotting, e.g., water spotting, mold, dirt, etc.

"Frontis foxed" means that the frontispiece is discolored by reddish brown markings that appear to be of the paper itself and not caused externally. Foxing occurs in papers as a result of the paper manufacturers' process sometimes being poorly handled, as in the bleaching process which promotes a chemical action over time that discolors parts, or all of the paper.

"T.p. v. sl. foxed" means that the title page is very slightly foxed.

"Text clean" means that the pages of the book containing text and illustrations (excepting the frontispiece) are not foxed, or soiled by dust or usage.

"Tight and fine." Tight means it is still tightly bound, no loose hinges or gatherings (sections of pages) separated from the spine.

"Not listed in Howes" refers to the bibliography of Americana, titled *U.S.iana* by Wright Howe, probably one of the most comprehensive bibliographies on Americana. *U.S.iana* is used by most curators and private collectors in building their Americana collections. Howe's use of "U.S.iana" instead of "Americana" as the title of his bibliography recognized that "America" traditionally meant all of the Americas, South, Central, and North, Mexico and Canada. However, Howe's designation of "U.S.iana" for books and related items of the United States of America, did not catch on, which is why Montana-iana, and Patagoniana, sometimes rub shoulders in some catalogues with Western, Southwestern, Northwestern, and so on, Americana.

That there are "other Upham titles in Howes," may or may not enhance the Upham title listed in the Moosabec Reach catalogue.

All serious beginners should own and consult reference books such as Carter's *ABC for Book Collectors* or the glossary of terms for the antiquarian and used used book trade published by *AB Bookman's Weekly*.

Sometimes book dealers will sell old auction catalogues which can still be useful to the collector. However, you may wish to subscribe to the rare book catalogues of sales conducted by auction houses. Auction house catalogues, with prices realized, are priced from five dollars; for a very significant collection going on the block, catalogue prices would be accordingly much higher.

Write to the auction houses requesting information on subscribing to their book auctions, or ask to be notified about book auctions in your specialty.

Some major book auction houses:

California Book Auction Galleries, 358 Golden Gate Avenue, San Francisco, CA 04102.

Sotheby Parke Bernet and Co., 1334 York Avenue, San Francisco, CA 94102.

Swann Galleries, 104 E. 25th Street, New York, NY 10010.

Investing/Collecting

For the past ten years surveys in the *Wall Street Journal* and by independent investment advisory services have placed rare books and manuscripts among the properties that are appreciating most rapidly in value.
  —Gordon N. Ray in his essay, "World of Rare Books Reexamined," *The Yale Library Gazette*

There is no price guide in this book. Book collecting price guides with "official" in their titles that are available in retail book outlets usually will have a disclaimer inside the cover. Prices of collectible books are subject to more variables than the prices of wheat futures. The condition of the book, its "points" (briefly, errors, misprints, changes of text, binding, any variants that determine [or allegedly determine] if it is a first or fifth printing), its scarcity, its demand, and so on.

A beginner who approaches a dealer with a price guide and, say, a copy of *Huckleberry Finn* in his hands, creates problems for himself and for the dealer. Even if it is the 1884 edition with E. W. Kemble's illustrations, it may have pages missing, or be indelibly stained. The condition of the book and its printing history (first printing of first edition, second?) needs to be considered.

A dealer must appraise the book. Most dealers charge for appraisals. Their fees vary. Ask beforehand. Some dealers are not experienced appraisers; some limit their appraising to private or institutional libraries; some are unfamiliar with any specialty other than their own.

Prices of books in any guide are drawn primarily from auction sales records. The auctioned book which your guide lists may have been in mint condition, may have come from the library of E. W. Howells, a friend and fellow writer, so it is an "association copy," adding to its value. The price paid may have been the result of frenzied bidding that sometimes arises in an auction room among bidders with more money than expertise, and the listed price may be unrealistic for that copy. Fees for auction sales can add twenty percent to the final auction price.

If your *Huckleberry Finn* is a fine copy and you demand the price listed in your guide, you are overlooking a small point but one that must loom large for the antiquarian dealer who must stay in business. If he does pay you the auction price, when he turns around to sell your copy to another customer, an experienced collector, what can the dealer charge him? What profit can he expect?

In any case, if you are serious about collecting, and not out to make a "killing," wait until you know more about collecting, have met and done business with more than one dealer who specializes in your interest, read as much as you can, visited shops, attended the antiquarian book fairs held in your area. You will be in a better position to judge the value of the books you own on their intrinsic merits and for their monetary value. You may decide to keep them as the core of your own collection.

If you are looking at book collecting for its "investment potential" only, then you are not really a book collector but a book speculator. Unless you are rich enough to afford those rarities—*Bay Psalm Book,* oldest known surviving book printed in America, of which there are less than a dozen copies; or Shakespeare's first folio editions, which are really museum pieces—you might do better to consider the stock market.

Some antiquarian dealers offer an "investment service" for individuals and groups. Using his own judgement, the dealer will develop a collection around a specialty, or willynilly, pick up books that he or she thinks show promise of increasing in value. The investors never see the books, in some cases, and the dealer is free to sell them if a profit can be realized, after which he or she will repeat the process. A dealer may offer this sort of "investment" service to customers since he is in business, presumably to make money, a not ignoble goal, and cannot turn away customers whatever their motives.

Two years ago, however, a firm in London shook the antiquarian book world by offering just such a service. The investor put down a minimum of a thousand dollars with which the dealer would buy books that appeared to be "good investments." The investor could avoid shipping costs by leaving his purchases with the dealer, where they presumably sat around his storeroom, appreciating like mad. After the initial flurry, "mostly from America" it was said, the responses dwindled although, at last report, the dealers at the firm were receiving inquiries from Arabs.

Most antiquarian book dealers deplore the speculative approach to collecting, or even the current emphasis on the investment aspect of collecting to the detriment of other, sounder aspects. One of the most disturbing consequences of book speculation is the possible distortion of a market that, except for the usual fads found in any market, is relatively stable. A stable market offers the serious collector, the institutional buyer for libraries and museums, research scholars, and the dealers themselves the opportunity to bring to bear on their collections and research the intelligence and discrimination necessary for the building of collections that will endure, benefiting future scholars and researchers.

The values of the commodity market are not those of the rare book trade. Subjecting books to the same frenzied speculation associated with pork belly futures means that people who are book-ignorant can elevate the worthless, corner the worthwhile, manipulate the market and create mistrust of and contempt for responsible dealers who resist.

When you collect books over a period of years, you come to understand that the occasional mistake a dealer makes will be inadvertent and every attempt is made to rectify it. Over the long course the dealer has given you more than you have paid for. He shares his knowledge, he encourages you in collecting a specialty that may not be popular, but that interests you. He helps you compile a checklist, recommends related reading, picks up books at estate and library sales that will enhance your collection. His understanding of the rationale of collecting aids you in focusing your collection so that it is coherent and of lasting value.

But the book speculator has no long term experience with the book dealer or the book market. He is not interested in books as books, but only as little money machines. When his purchases do not appreciate fast enough in the books-as-commodities market, he will blame the dealer.

Books do appreciate in value; they also depreciate, or hold steady for decades.

Books artificially inflated in an "up" market might be considered non-liquid assets in a "down" market. Knowledgeable dealers will not pursue a specialty they sense is levelling out, no matter how frenzied the activity among inexperienced dealers or book speculators. A book may be a very nice book, worth a certain price, and deserving the attention of collectors. Those who created and fanned an artificial demand for it did not do it any favors. They gave it a bad reputation as a "flash in the pan," making serious collectors wary.

So, when you call on a dealer, leave your price guide at home.

The antiquarian dealer consults, among other guides, the *American Book Prices Current*, and *Gale's Price Guide*. Their cost is considerably more than the price guide you or I would buy in a retail outlet. Interpreting the prices in these guides demands a thorough knowledge of books, and the book markets of the past, the present, and some awareness of future trends.

But it is his own knowledge of the books he buys and sells, his judgement, honed by years of experience and sometimes, even as in science, it is a hunch about a certain book, or direction in collecting, that ultimately influences the price he pays or sets.

Consult your own interests and taste in collecting. You need not discuss your subject with anyone but your dealer. Come to think of it, one of the delights of book collecting is that you don't need a lot of people around, nor do you need to justify why you collect or what you collect, although it is fun to hear a collector talk about his specialty. When a collector talks about his books he is never boring, however pedestrian his views on other subjects.

Another satisfying aspect of collecting is how quickly you can become an expert in your specialty, particularly if it is a new area of collecting, and not popular. If the specialty you choose is popular, it will be more expensive to collect. If it is of no interest to you and you collect it merely because it is popular, it will be just an expensive affectation.

A sudden spurt of activity in a subject or an author (and "sudden" in the antiquarian book world can mean over a ten year period) happens when collectors in several different specialties see in another author or subject, works that will fit naturally into their collections.

Willa Cather has enjoyed a steady, unspectacular popularity among collectors who rightly consider her a major figure in American literature. Her works have been collected for years, and the serious collector wants every issue of each work, not just the first editions. They want the beautifully illustrated extract from *Death Comes for the Archbishop* which was printed in a very limited edition as Christmas presents for the author's friends, as well as her article, "My First Novels (There Were Two)," that appeared in *Colophon, Part 6,* in 1931.

Miss Cather's books turn up sometimes at used book sales, but not in large numbers. Unlike many American authors collected like big game, Cather inspires a strong loyalty in her collectors; she braces us.

Young readers are seeking her out. Weary of the writers to whom the young are supposed to "relate," they are turning to the writers scorned as "old-fashioned" or "irrelevant to our needs" by teachers who have never read them.

Miss Cather is honored by other American writers. E. B. White, Thurber, and others called her "The Olympian." Sinclair Lewis, first American to win the Nobel Prize in literature, said he would have preferred to have written *Death Comes for the Archbishop.* Miss Cather is esteemed internationally for her classicism and strength. Aside from the acknowledged excellence of her writing (which, nevertheless, was cavalierly dismissed by Edmund Wilson as "minor"; Wilson had many blind spots despite his critical gifts), Cather is of interest to the collector because she can be sought for many different specialties outside of author category.

Collector interest in the Southwest is booming, and *Death Comes for the Archbishop* is a splendid account of the uneasy, sometimes violent encounter of the European sensibility with the Indian and Mexican cultures, and the rootless, cultureless white American presence in the Southwest. *The Professor's House* contains the haunting story of Tom Outland's discovery of the green mesa, the great pueblo city in the Southwest. Collector of Canadiana would want *Shadow on the Rock,* the brooding story of French emigres clinging, in a frozen wilderness, to the culture of an indifferent mother country. Specialists in the development of musical artists on the American frontier would wish to own *Song of the Lark* or *Lucy Gayheart.*

The resurgence of feminism in the past few decades makes Cather sought after by collectors of American women writers—although Cather's breadth of vision and disciplined intellect made her incapable of depicting her people, men or women, as victims. Her sculptor (*The Sculptor's Funeral*) triumphs in death over his squalid origins, and even Paul (*Paul's Case*) in a queer way confounds those depressingly practical realists determined to force him to adjust to a world that horrifies him. Collectors of writings on architecture would want, in fiction, Cather's first novel, *Alexander's Bridge,* which is very scarce.

Competing with all these specialties is the collector of the book, as book, for its printing and design. Cather's books benefited from her association with her second publisher, the young Alfred Knopf. Knopf was extraordinary as a publisher, combining an instinct for excellence in writing with an appreciation of type design, papers, binding; Knopf books are sought by some collectors regardless of author.

I am not suggesting that anyone should collect Cather, or predicting an imminent rise in the prices of her books. I discuss Miss Cather's work to show that where price is concerned, tastes, competing specialties, fashion and scarcity determine what the collector will pay, more than the price listed for one volume in a price guide.

We should all range wide in our reading, not slavishly following trends, or trying to keep up with the best-seller lists. Most of the very best writing, the important ideas of today, never make it to the best-seller list. But even with an ever narrowing margin of profit, some publishers still publish books that they know will not be big sellers. Some of them are the books that will redeem us from the future's harsh judgement.

In the blizzard of non-books, books of lasting value, beautifully made books are being published. These are the books that will appreciate, that are already appreciating.

It is vital that we read in the past; but we should avoid thinking of collectible books as relics of the past. Good books from the past are here today because people in the past—their present—recognized their worth and saved them for the future.

Antiquarian Book Fairs

Antiquarian book fairs are held locally, regionally, and nationally throughout the year. For the beginning collector they offer the opportunity to meet antiquarian book dealers who specialize in the collector's own interest, or to discover specialties they may not have considered. Collectors, novice and expert, study the books that will enhance their collections.

The interest in books, and in book collecting, has never been higher, and this interest cuts across social and economic classes. New paths are being opened by new collectors. Most antiquarian and used-book dealers have a sincere desire to bring the beginning collector into the antiquarian book world. Unfortunately, there seems at present to be no consistent approach to doing this.

In one breath, some dealers lament the absence of the beginning collector at these fairs and lately, the absence of experienced collectors, and in the next breath the same dealers sneer at the "lookers, questioners, and touchers" who show up at the fairs and dismiss the novice as a "failed English major" or "bored housewife wanting a free appraisal of granny's bible." But the majority of antiquarian dealers are uncomfortable with these attitudes that chill the beginner's zeal. They realize that every experienced collector was once a beginner struggling through the abbreviations in dealers' catalogues.

How to make these fairs more attractive to the beginner without discouraging attendance of the institutional buyer and long-term collector is an issue the committees for the fairs are addressing. The Ephemera Society of America conferences, for instance, feature lively discussion groups for both beginners and experts, lectures, exhibits, and a general atmosphere of friendliness.

The more cosmopolitan fairs are generally held in fine old hotels such as the Ambassador in San Francisco and the Copley Plaza in Boston. Logic, not snobbery, dictates this site selection. Such hotels do not have huge lobbies of the Airport Functional school of architecture, with their frenetic activity, boring decor, and a half dozen conventions and rallies going on in cavernous, Astro-turfed "function rooms." The management and staff of these fine downtown hotels are experienced in providing effective settings and security for specialized shows such as antique, fine gemstones, and book fairs. Such shows have far different requirements than large manufacturers' trade shows.

The Copley Plaza, for example, has marble floors, oriental carpets, spatterings of stained glass. Built in a time when moire or velvet bound dance cards were filled in by young men in evening dress for popular beauties or their dismal cousins, the Copley Plaza's ballroom has crystal chandeliers and a spaciousness that is more than just space. When the ballroom is filled with books from all over the world, there is an almost unbearable excitement in the air as you enter. The glimmer of gold leaf, the scent of calf, and the colorful dust jackets are, to us, more potent arousers of desire than the trinkets, fragrances, and Worth ball gowns of the past.

There should be a receiving line at these hotel fairs, so the giddy or shy have time to arrange their disordered enthusiasms. Perhaps dance cards should be distributed with suggestions from the dealers, so that a book whose sterling worth is presently dimmed by flashy best-sellers everyone seems to covet, will not be overlooked.

Dealers bring dismal cousins along to the ballrooms because they know what time and experience will teach the beginner: that books, like people, are fated to be cast aside if their worth is calculated only in terms of how many people lust after them at a given point in time.

You need not be a millionaire to be a collector, but the objects of your connoisseurship deserve the finest setting. The collector, beginner and expert alike, must view them, talk about them, think about them in an unhurried atmosphere. Thinking about books, the desired ones, is not like thinking about anything else. I have heard people compare it with the ruminations of romantic love, even to listing points. I don't agree. You don't really think about a person you are attracted to. That person just affects you differently than, say, your mother, or any number of people that wander in and out of your life. The person may encumber your imagination for a while, but the possibility of exercising intelligent curiosity or rational analysis toward the person is absent.

But you do think about books, and though there is the longing, hope, and despair that is associated with romantic love, the consequences of a misalliance can be more immediately dismaying. The suspicious dust jacket, the missing point, are no less dispiriting than the lover who whips out an emery board and begins filing his or her nails in your favorite French restaurant. A book's defects are not things your infatuation permits you to overlook.

Dealers suggest that beginners attend these fairs, ask questions, examine the books. It is to the dealer's advantage to encourage the beginner. Incidentally, it will be very helpful for a person new to book collecting if he or she, perhaps previous to attending antiquarian book fairs, has read a few books on collecting, and managed to get a dealer's catalogue such as the one, for example, published by Moosabec Reach Historical Company, Book and Print Department of the Jonesport Wood Company, Jonesport, Maine. This catalogue gives the beginner a fighting chance both by explaining the abbreviations used in describing the books offered, and including a comprehensive bibliography of references.

Unfortunately, there seems to be one dealer at least, at every fair, who spurns the new collector, ignoring his questions or answering abruptly while searching the room for the institutional buyers or book speculators who buy "two of everything that's hot."

Lately, however, the institutional buyer is back in his office struggling with a request to the trustees for funds simply to repair and maintain a collection expanded, perhaps too rapidly, in the recent, well-funded past. And the speculator, facing a cash-flow problem of his own, may be in his banker's office learning the hard facts about non-liquid assets in a soft economy.

But our dealer, undaunted, will make it clear he did not travel to the fair to waste time with anyone who does not approach his booth with checkbook out and a hotel porter at his side to haul away his purchases. Ignoring the students who ask about the Hemingway in the display case, sneering at the young woman who refers to "unopened" pages as "uncut," and successfully intimidating fairgoers whose pretensions are not as grand as his own. If he is the first dealer approached by the novice, his behavior will have a poor effect on the sales and future prospects of the other exhibitors.

People will cheerfully take all sorts of self-improvement courses and not consider themselves worthless because their "life skills" need improving. But there is something profoundly disturbing about appearing stupid or unrefined before those we think of as "brainy" or "cultured." We will go to almost any lengths to avoid the humiliation that might result from such an encounter.

This self-imposed limitation on our natural curiosity is, I think, the most tragic aspect of our native derangements about caste and class. It may be the result of our immigrant past, or of a racial memory of high priests and wizards and their monopoly of the word, printed on paper or pressed on clay, or it may be the insanity of an educational system that pits child against child.

When a person does make the effort to overcome his reluctance to expose his lack of knowledge, he does so hoping he will not be judged, once again, unworthy. When a bookseller squelches that hope and that curiosity, he betrays his calling and degrades the idea of the book.

I would like to see a beginners' exhibit—or several exhibits—centering on different specialties: 19th century authors, modern children's books by author or illustrator, children's miniature books past and present, crime and detective fiction, sports fiction, for example.

In his *Dreaming of Heroes: American Sports Fiction, 1868-1980*, published by Nelson-Hall, Michael V. Oriard reminds us that 70 million viewers watch the Super Bowl. That's a lot of potential collectors of Frank Merriwell. *Dreaming* comes with a checklist of American sports fiction and a bibliography.

Dealers could assemble small beginner "kits" in their specialties including "working copies" to highlight the more valuable copies. Beginner reading lists in particular specialties could be made up and distributed. The kits might even be sold.

Lectures for beginners should be offered. More experienced collectors could be asked to discuss their collections and, more to the point, how they started collecting, their mistakes, and what they learned from them, in workshops for beginners.

Whenever I attend a fair and see dealers talking to other dealers while diffident, obvious beginners try to get their attention, nervously apologizing for bothering them, I wonder, what is the point of these fairs? Why could not some hours during the fair be reserved for beginners? Why not have tours of the exhibition booths with exhibitors prepared to discuss their specialties in terms the beginner can understand? Why not a cocktail party for new collectors, or a luncheon with speakers, dealers and experienced collectors who could truly welcome beginners?

Advertising for the fairs might include notices of beginner activities. Display sheets could be sent to libraries and bookshops. Local antiquarian dealers in the cities and towns where the fairs are to be held could contact radio and television stations far enough ahead to appear on "talk shows" using displays that can easily be discussed.

Many beginning collectors attend antiquarian book fairs, but few are noticed. Really encouraging the beginner to attend and benefit from these events need not compromise the dignity of the dealers, and would enhance the overall value of the event for all concerned. There are enormously rewarding areas within which the dealer and new collector can meet.

Antiquarian and used-book dealers can tell you when these fairs are being held in your area.

The Collector's Reference Shelf

෴

Books

ABC FOR BOOK COLLECTORS, by John Carter. Alfred A. Knopf, rev. ed. 1963, $11.95.

ABC contains more than 450 definitions of terms of the antiquarian trade. The sometimes baffling abbreviatons and descriptions used in dealer and auction house catalogues are explained and analyzed (some to the length of several pages). Carter was a witty, sometimes irreverent lexicographer, but his scholarship was impeccable.

Educated at Eton and at King's College, Cambridge, Carter was a member of the Sadleir Circle, a name given to a group of London dealers and collectors that set new standards of bibliographic exactness for the antiquarian trade.

Carter wrote and edited books about books, and with Percy Muir, another Circle member, edited *Printing and the Mind of Man*, a compilation of what are considered the major printed works that significantly affected the history of ideas, since the invention of moveable type.

The *ABC for Book Collectors* should be in every collector's reference library. Older editions (there have been five since the first in 1952) occasionally turn up at used booksellers, but not often.

COLLECTIBLE BOOKS: SOME NEW PATHS, edited by Jean Peters. R. R. Bowker Co., 1979, $16.95.

Peters states in the preface that her book is not intended for beginners, as it lacks "definitions of terms, descriptions of how a book is put together," etc. But I believe that beginners are intimidated by too much technical information that in many cases is written with the assumptions that the beginner is already familiar with the jargon of the trade, and that the technical aspects are what draws the new beginner to collecting. This is hardly the case.

What fascinates the beginner, as the experienced collector, is a love of books and a desire to know more about them: what makes certain books fascinating to some people, how books reflect and perhaps influence social conditions, why people collect contemporary books, how to collect books in a specialty that is not popular and for which there is no bibliography. The writers take up these questions with clarity and style.

Charles Gullans and John Espey contributed "American Trade Bindings and Their Designers, 1880-1915," a brief but thorough history of artists and the book bindings they designed during that period when decorative book bindings were most popular. This has not been a heavily collected specialty, although it is becoming increasingly popular, so there have been no definitive or even nearly complete bibliographies on these artists and their works to which a collector could refer.

In searching for examples of the work of artist Margaret Armstrong, Gullans and Espey became true detectives in gathering, evaluating, keeping and discarding evidence for Armstrong's works, much of it unsigned and unrecorded by the publishers of the books Armstrong's exquisite art embellished.

Gullans and Espey show the beginner how a bibliography is formed, and the way one is caught up in the excitement of the chase, the chase in which the developing bibliography on Armstrong is as suspenseful and satisfying as any of the scattered clues in a mystery story.

G. Thomas Tanselle writes sympathetically and knowledgeably about collecting non-firsts. To the beginner who may think of collectible books as being old books and only first editions, Tanselle's championing of the virtues of non-firsts will be an agreeable surprise. To the collector who has invested heavily, and perhaps indiscriminately in "firsts," Tanselle's essay might not be so agreeable.

"Film Books" by Daniel Leab shows the beginner who may not trust his own taste how an invaluable collection can be built around a personal interest that may not seem at present to be a worthwhile specialty. Leab began collecting books on movies when there was little interest in this subject as a collectible area. He was able to buy books cheaply and eventually sold his collection to the Australian National Library.

Leab did not collect for profit; the size of his collection, the expenses of insurance and proper maintenance influenced his decision to sell what had begun as a collection based on a personal interest and pursued for pleasure. He advises the collector, "There is a need for specialization on the part of those now beginning as collectors in this field . . . . The beauty of collecting books about film is that no approach is exclusive and that any is valid provided it has some intellectual coherence." Movie fans might wish to collect books and related materials around the movies, directors, or stars that are their favorites, or around favorite subjects, western movies or movies about outer space.

Leab is author of *Sambo to Superspade: The Black Experience in Motion Pictures* (Boston, Houghton Mifflin, 1975).

"American Mass Market Paperbacks" is contributed by Thomas L. Bonn. Bonn discusses how respectable collections might be shaped from the swarms of mass market paperbacks, and though some may remain unconvinced, Bonn brings a discriminating intelligence to bear on the subject. He points out that valuable paperbacks might include famous authors whose works first appeared in paperback—Kurt Vonnegut, William Burroughs, John D. McDonald, early science fiction novels and mystery and detective stories.

Peter B. Howard's article, "American Fiction Since 1960," would reinforce what was learned from Tanselle in de-mystifying the collecting of first editions.

Howard's discussion of publishers' attempts to distort the purpose of collecting in this specialty, through greed and through ignorance of the real purpose of collecting, can teach the beginner a great deal about the hazards of "high spot" collecting.

Percy Muir's "The Sadleir Circle in Perspective" introduces the beginner to many of the people who helped shape standards for modern collecting.

I recommend this book to the serious beginner. The reference material listed after each article is invaluable.

Bowker books can be order by credit card on their toll-free number: 1-800-521-8110, or by mail: R. R. Bowker, Order Department, P.O. Box 1807, Ann Arbor, MI 48106.

Periodicals

AB BOOKMAN'S WEEKLY, P.O. Box AB, Clifton, NJ 07015. A year's subscription is $50 bulk mail U.S. ($55 outside U.S.). First class is $85 U.S., Canada, Mexico. The subscription, in addition to the *Weekly* (including special issues), also includes the two-part *AB Bookman's Yearbook*. Current single copies of the *Weekly* are $5, special issues $6.

I consider this the single most important reference source for the serious beginning collector. It is the antiquarian and used-book dealer's bible, but the breadth and depth of the essays about books and collecting written by collectors, dealers, and curators of rare and scholarly collections, among others, makes it indispensable to the beginning collector's education.

It is not so difficult to learn how to collect books, but learning why books should be collected and preserved is sometimes more elusive.

Whether it is William Reese (antiquarian dealer, New Haven, Connecticut) writing of Archibald Hanna, Curator of Western Americana at Yale University's Beinecke Library, or Frederick R. Goff, retired Chief of the Rare Books Department of the Library of Congress, the writers in *AB Bookman's Weekly* sistent and determined efforts of Archie Hanna to create a research collection both broad and deep") or Frederick R. Goff, retired Chief of the Rare Books Department of the Library of Congress, the writers in *A B Bookman's Weekly* show to what purpose the thoughtful collector gathers books.

The *Weekly* carries pages of want lists—books wanted by dealers, university and private libraries, and collectors. There are also pages of books for sale by dealers and private parties that can help the beginning collector learn about what to look for in his or her specialty and current prices being asked.

AB Bookman's Weekly publishes special issues devoted to specific collecting specialties: crime literature, Western Americana, children's books, paper ephemera, etc.

The *Weekly* advertises local, regional, and national antiquarian book fairs. Sponsors of the larger used-book sales, libraries and colleges advertise their sales in the *Weekly*.

AMERICAN BOOK COLLECTOR, 274 Madison Avenue, New York, NY 10016. Published bi-monthly; a year's subscription is $16.50.

The *American Book Collector* has informative articles on collecting trends and specialties and about people in the trade. It provides an invaluable service to the collector with its continuing checklists of titles for specific collections. Its bibliographical information in these checklists is thorough.

ABC discusses trends in collecting, provides information on coming events, and lists the publication of dealers' latest catalogues.

Collecting Books
for the Home Library

In a recent article in *The New Yorker* magazine, William F. Buckley, Jr. mentioned going into a house where there were no books. It was apparently a disquieting experience, as it is for most people who live in a house where books live. There are houses that contain books, the latest best sellers, sets of encyclopedias, or chunks of book club reprints breaking up shelf space between reproductions of African masks and pre-Columbian pots, but books do not live there, either. It is a queer feeling to sense that however pleasant and personable the people who occupy these houses are, there is a chasm of difference in perception and outlook between them and the true reader that even mutual affection and respect cannot bridge.

People who live in houses where books live are true readers. They are not necessarily more intelligent than those who are not, but their thinking usually has a depth, breadth and sympathy that may be absent in those who read to get the facts or to be conversationally up-to-date and aware of current social and literary trends.

True readers are not so concerned about facts as they are about the ideas concerning the facts. They do not disdain new writers, but are just as excited about writers from every period. They cannot read enough of Surtees, if they are lucky enough to find him, and *Handley Cross* is never far from hand; Mr. John Jorrocks resolves all their own ego problems with, "What a huntsman I should be if it were not for the leaps." They will read Nabokov's *Speak Memory* and Juan Goytisolo's *Juan the Landless* and be moved by compassion in both instances. True readers are curious; they do not limit their reading to what others have said is "great" and must be read seriatim according to a plan that when completed will mark them as "well read."

They are not so interested in being well read as in reading well and widely. They have a passion to learn everything about anything that sparks their imaginations. So, *Our Birds in Their Haunts* shares shelf space with *The Decline and Fall of the Roman Empire* and Jane Austen finds herself next to *The Jesuits in North America*. Margaret Fuller is stranded next to Washington Irving's *Astoria*, and what is Tom Lorenz's *Guys Like Us* doing there lounging against Tolstoy's *The Cossacks?*

It is not mere whimsy to say that books live in houses, it is a fact, a sometimes discouraging fact to those who have an inordinate desire to tidy things up. The most dispiriting thing that can happen to a true reader is to come home to a tidy house. All day he or she has been looking forward to going through the stack of botany books or small press poetry books, bought for a song at a used-book sale, and left on the floor by a favorite armchair.

After the first shock of tidiness, the true reader pulls the new prizes off the shelves and gets back to the real business of coming home. But he or she can't remember how the other books, not in the original stack, got on the kitchen counter or into someone else's chair. The true reader is as baffled by roaming books as the non-true reader with whom he or she shares the tidy house.

There are many books from many different countries and periods, and about many different subjects, in the true reader's library. True readers are daring, and do not limit themselves to the known and safe.

In building a fine home library of sound titles, we should be like the true reader—adventurous. To be adventurous is to go back to the classics we think we are familiar with because we recognize the titles or the names of the authors. We should read them again, not as an exercise in "lit crit" but in order to be fully engaged with the author without having to worry about interpreting each line according to a "correct approach," and in a jargon that seems beyond the uninitiated.

College students who are not English majors get the message early on in required English courses that the study of literature is an arcane enterprise. The devotees of the cult of literature as "language and nothing else" with its emphasis on form and symbolism, primarily Freudian, have made literature an arid orthodoxy. Unfortunately, students who are repelled by this orthodoxy tend to blame themselves for lacking the proper aesthetic temperament. They may come to believe that literature is "above" them, and mistrust their own ability to understand and enjoy it.

After all, if a book stirs them intellectually and emotionally, if they are enchanted by Anna's plump hands flickering over the things on her dressing table, or laugh when Vronsky says, "Oh, the darling" to his mare going over a jump, they are obviously missing the point. They should be paying attention to the number of commas Tolstoy used and why Vronsky chose a mare to ride.

Van Wyck Brooks in his *The Writer in America* (E.P. Dutton, 1953) discusses the deadening effect of this orthodoxy on American writing and writers. This orthodoxy is still firmly in place in many college English departments. *The Writer in America* is a healthy antidote to the excesses of this orthodoxy, and gives the reader a sounder perspective on literature. Brooks is still scorned in many English departments because he insists that literature is not a pseudo-science accessible only to a tiny elite.

Brooks also wrote *Makers and Finders: A History of the Writer in America 1800-1915* (E.P. Dutton). The five volumes that make up this work—*The World of Washington Irving, The Flowering of New England, The Times of Melville and Whitman, New England: Indian Summer,* and *The Confident Years: 1885-1915*—can be picked up book by book, or in the entire series at used-book shops and library sales for less than one dollar a copy, depending on the printing. I had to pay four dollars for my copy of *The Writer in America* but it was a first edition in dust jacket. For the home library builder searching for American writers, Brooks's *Makers and Finders* series is indispensable. Brooks sought out writers famous and obscure, going back to the earliest days of the Union, including some forgotten in the bustle of the young nation's expansion.

Brooks aroused the wrath of many members of the literary establishment by calling his series a "literary history." They objected because the series was not about the history of literary forms. Brooks was unusually sensitive to his critics; he appears to have had more respect for them than they deserved. Their attacks on his landmark work, *The Ordeal of Mark Twain*, aggravated a depression so severely that Brooks stopped writing for several years. Fortunately for America, Brooks recovered and continued the formidable task of rediscovering America's literary past. The *Makers and Finders* series is not only an example of Brooks's impeccable scholarship, it is written in a lively and thoroughly readable style. It can be used as a checklist for specialty collectors and those wishing to expand their home library's American writers section.

The literature of America, unlike the literatures of other countries, has almost disappeared. Students and teachers alike must scramble to find works of American writers to use in college English classes. Cheap, paperback reprints are sometimes unavailable in sufficient numbers and have small, almost unreadable type on brittle, easily torn paper. If students wish to read other works by an author being studied in class, they are soon discouraged by the difficulty of obtaining lesser known works in any format.

The lack of affordable and well-made books by Hawthorne, Irving, Twain, Poe, Prescott, and other American writers will not be remedied by the much-heralded publication of the Library of America series. College English teachers may rejoice that their students will have a "textually correct" book containing three of Herman Melville's romances on acid-free paper, but the students and their parents cannot be expected to cheer at the $25.00 price tag on each book, nor will the true reader be especially entranced.

The Library of America received preliminary funding to publish American classics from the Ford Foundation ($600,000) and from the National Endowment for the Humanities ($1,200,000). An earlier NEH grant to the Modern Language Association (the professional association of college and university English teachers) did little towards getting readable texts of American classics to the American public whose taxes supposedly were being used to that end.

In 1968, Edmund Wilson proposed a cheap, readable collection of American literature such as the collection of France's literature published by Gallimard in Paris. After the initial government grant to the Modern Language Association, Wilson observed what he considered to be an MLA boondoggle and expressed his disgust in a letter to the *New York Review of Books.* He wrote, "The editing of the classical American writers has got to be an academic racket that is coming between these writers and the public to which they ought to be accessible.

Wilson's letter sparked a war of words between those who wanted American classics made available inexpensively to American readers, and those who appeared to consider the American classics their own private industry that the "unlettered masses" would be permitted to subsidize. In a pamphlet, "The Fruits of the MLA" printed by the *New York Review of Books,* Wilson discussed what he considered the MLA's perversion of his original idea for a collection of American classics. The pamphlet also contains quotations from letters of graduate students working on the project which Wilson considered cynical and which fueled his outrage.

The Library of America is leasing some of the MLA texts from this period for a percentage of the royalties. Because of the supposedly significant changes made by the MLA and by graduate students, these texts are considered new creations and are copyrighted. All other editions of the same American classics remain in the public domain.

It would be unfortunate if English teachers demanded that students use the Library of America texts exclusively, or only MLA approved texts. The occasional variations in older editions available in used-book shops could be dealt with briefly in class and the instructor could get on with the essentials, unless he considers misplaced commas what literature is about.

The earliest editions are closer to the intentions of the author since the author usually went over the galleys personally. It can be assumed, in most cases, that the author was satisfied. To throw up a thicket of jargon that presumes to carve into stone an institutional explanation of what the author really intended to say, or should have or would have said if he had been properly conditioned by the institution, is to further distance the reader from the intentions of the original author.

Students should not be denied the right to use older editions of American classics because of variants that do not alter the substance of the writers' work, and are of only narrow bibliographical interest. A national literature with only one officially correct interpretation will bring death to the living tradition of American writing more swiftly than neglect.

Students forced to accept "official" texts might be terrified in later years at the sight of Parkman's histories in the handsome Riverside Edition; or of the stamped signature set of Twain's works, twenty-six volumes in their beautiful green and gilt bindings. These sets, and sets of Hawthorne, Irving, Prescott, Melville, Poe, and other American writers can be found at used-book shops and sales for less than $25.00, and for considerably less in the closing hours of a used-book sale. Buy these books for your home library, for your children and for their children. Many of these sets were printed on acid-free, quality paper that is not disintegrating.

American literature exists within the framework of the Western cultural tradition, of Greece and Rome and the literature of England and Europe. Perhaps the most important contribution to the growth of Western culture and to universal literacy was the protestant reformation. The idea that the individual Christian was responsible for his own salvation required that the keys to understanding Christianity be turned over to the individual. For Christians, the Bible contained the keys and access to them could be gained only by learning to read.

The language of the Bible permeates our literature and our common speech —the prodigal son, the silver cord, the mess of pottage, the garden of Eden, the mark of Cain. The humanities may be a sinking landscape, more and more withdrawn from the common life that nourished it in the past, but these phrases are still recognized, however dimly, as having meaning for us. Our understanding of Western culture and history would be distorted if we assumed that the Bible was no more than a set of religious documents for Jews and Christians. But except for college level courses on the Bible as literature, the Bible as a force in Western history and culture is generally ignored.

A young college student whose early training in Hebrew school had inspired in him a love of literature, especially poetry, told me of an instructor in one of his classes who was unable to discuss the biblical context of the phrases previously mentioned, or that of literary titles such as *The Sun Also Rises* and *The Golden Bowl*. The instructor had attributed the saying, "Where there is no vision the people perish," to a politician whose own vision continues to be questioned.

The antipathy felt by many people towards the use of the Bible in public schools to propagate religion at taxpayer expense should not extend to the Bible itself. The King James version of the Bible should be in every home library; it contains the finest examples of the English language at its vigorous and lyrical best.

No school of literary criticism, however powerful its hold on the academic community, can assure us that only their pet writers are worthy of exclusive study for all time. In *The Writer in America*, Van Wyck Brooks writes, "Every generation makes its own choices of the past." But many, students and nonstudents, lack confidence in their own intelligence and discernment when their personal choices in literature do not follow the "official" line. An early familiarity with literature in our home libraries will help to remedy this diffidence.

It is important to read in the past, to have those books in the home library that show us how rich and varied that past is. However, it is just as important to read in the present, and not just the works of those writers who currently enjoy celebrity. Nearly twenty percent of all fiction published in the United States is

published by the small, independent presses. These publishers take chances on new writers whose styles and points of view are, in many cases, original and highly individualistic.

The small presses in the past nurtured many now famous writers, including Hemingway, James Joyce, William Carlos Williams, Marianne Moore, Louise Bogan. Their writings were considered too strange; the commercial publishers of their time feared they might prove difficult or troubling to the reader, whom the publishers assumed wanted what was familiar and safe.

Today's small presses are providing the same outlets for fiction, nonfiction and poetry from all regions of the country and the world. America is not only Los Angeles and New York City; the American experience is not the travesty of American life that those who fly between New York City and Los Angeles put on television.

Most American writers are not celebrities; they do not haunt television talk shows, or give long, self-important interviews to newspapers and magazines. They have not yet become parodies of their media images so they are not hustled for their opinions on politics, art, crime or tap-dancing, nor are they bagged to appear at conferences on the declining state of literature. Most American writers stay home in Iowa, New Mexico, California, North Carolina, Texas, or Maine, and they do what writers are supposed to do. They write.

Sanford Phippen is a high-school teacher in Maine who reviews books for *Maine Life* magazine. Phippen, a native of Maine, sees that state through the eyes of the native and knows how the non-native sees Maine and the natives. Since most visitors to Maine come for its beauty and its opportunities for sport and relaxation, they rarely see what Phippen calls "the Maine that's missing." What is missing from the popular literature about Maine is the high rate of alcoholism, the low wages, primitive housing and other grimmer aspects of Maine life. Nor are visitors pleased when these things are described, as Phippen learned from the reaction to his published articles and a public radio broadcast about "the Maine that's missing."

Phippen is a strong writer, and in his collection of short stories *The Police Know Everything* (Puckerbrush Press, 1982) we see him with the natives, his people, in "Sister's Wedding Had a Lot of Firsts," "Death of a Lobster Truck Driver," and "The Return of the Maine Native." In "Cocktails on the Point," he is in "enemy" territory, and the non-natives do not bother to conceal their contempt for his people.

Phippen's stories are not "Maine-type" stories with the familiar mythic Mainers—strong, taciturn, wise and witty, proud but folksy. Stereotypes are born of the observer's condescension, his fear and ignorance of those observed. It is much easier to deal with stereotypes than with Phippen's real people. With stereotypes we can chuckle or grow misty-eyed over their follies and ignorance of the real world, while ignoring their world and, conveniently for us, their humanity.

Phippen writes of one region of America, and the American experience in that region. But his writing transcends the regional, and the claim his people make on our shared humanity stays with us. This is true of other American writers who write of the American experience in their regions, and whether their region is Harlem, the Texas Panhandle, or the Rocky Mountains, these writers enlarge our understanding not just of their region, but of the larger world.

In many writing classes the emphasis seems to be on "slanting" writing to a particular magazine or even to a particular editor. There are even lessons on "finding saleable plots" and how to get characters to move from one room to another. Small press writers, while observing the forms of grammar and syntax, do not buy the "Tinker-toy" theory of writing. Their writing is not slanted but intensely personal, fresh and surprising. The reader responds, laughs, nods, or is suddenly very still. These writers speak in their own voices, and the true reader wants to hear these voices again and again, for they say the things we need to know.

But small press books and magazines are unobtainable at most bookstores. The present distribution system does not allow for the sound titles of even the large publishers to remain on the shelves if they are not fast movers. Some used-book shops and public libraries have begun stocking small press books and sponsoring readings by writers appearing in small presses. More libraries and used-book shops should do this, for a distribution system that rejects these works is no less deadening than a political tyranny if it results in the suppression of ideas.

Small presses have formed associations in different parts of the country and are working to get their books to readers. Many of these associations issue catalogues such as the "Maine Book Catalogue/Sampler" put out by the Maine Writers and Publishers Alliance. Their catalogue is free on request from MWPA, Box 7542 dts, Portland, ME 04112.

Readers can learn more about the offerings of small presses by reading the annual (there have been six so far) *Pushcart Prize: Best of the Small Presses* volumes edited by Bill Henderson and published by the Pushcart Press (P.O. Box 380, Wainscott, NY 11975). The Pushcart Prize was established in 1976 by a group of writers that included Anais Nin, Buckminster Fuller, Joyce Carol Oates, Ralph Ellison, Reynolds Price, and Ishmael Reed, whose works were first published in small press editions. Small press- and little magazine-published essays, poetry, short stories, and excerpts from novels are nominated for consideration each year and those selected form the one volume collection.

Many libraries have *The Pushcart Prize*, but if yours does not you can request it from the state library through your local library. The small presses from which the selections were drawn are listed, as well as a list of notable small presses. The *Pushcart Prize* also contains works of the underground press in Russia, and the works of writers from Europe, Latin America, Asia and Africa.

Small presses give the true reader the opportunity to read authors who, though unknown today, may be recognized in the future as major contributors to our literary heritage.

Home Library for Children

Dictionaries, almanacs, and encyclopedias (available at used-book shops and sales) can be kept in a common area, but children should have their own library of books they have chosen for themselves. Their books should be in their own rooms or in a special place in a shared room, kept in old crates if that is all that can be managed.

It may be convenient for writers and their publishers to assign chronological categories to children's books, but children should not be forced to limit their reading to these categories. The great classic children's books such as *Gulliver's Travels* and *Robinson Crusoe* were written for adults, but adopted by children in an age when books were not written specifically for children.

It is not necessary for every child to read what every other child is reading at the same age. Age groupings deny the dizzying variety of children's interests and their natural abilities.

Adults who buy gift books for children should not be hedged by arbitrary limitations, spurning books about dinosaurs or clouds that are of passionate interest to the child who is unaware of the artificial barriers surrounding his or her curiosity. Children's zeal to know about everything that catches their fancy will launch them past the "difficult" words.

Parents should not worry when a child stumbles in reading. Readers of all ages, like runners, stumble occasionally, but we do not tell runners to stop running until they can do it flawlessly. Putting a book away until a child is "ready" for it is a waste. Reading readiness is as meaningless a concept as breathing readiness. When children are ready, according to the experts, their interest might have been usurped by video games.

Children live with the knowledge that they are at the mercy of adults, those big bodies that are always crashing around them. I think that is why children are fascinated by dinosaurs; their hugeness and menace are safely extinct. Children want to go where the dinosaur bones are buried, dig them up, check them out. The big bodies in a child's world are always in great haste to perpetuate the tedium of their own existence by teaching children what they think every child should know.

A child should know only the things that child, at a particular time, wants to know. If children are lucky enough to have retained that pristine snobbery from the time when they ignored the new toy in favor of the box it came in, they will reject the books that coyly tell them how to be better citizens, friends, sandcastle builders, and so on. Children must re-invent the wheel to their own satisfaction, not to the specifications of helpful adults. Adults should stay out of the way of a child's understanding of the world, and not interpret what the child reads. That robs children of their right to their own experiences.

A young parent, hoping to instill in his child values the parent found soothing, reminded his child of Mr. Wonka's cruel test of Charlie in *Charlie and the Chocolate Factory* by Roald Dahl (Alfred A. Knopf, New York, 1964). The parent explained to his son that given the dreadful circumstances of Charlie's life, Charlie would have been justified in betraying Mr. Wonka, who was rich and powerful.

Happily, the son passionately rejected this bit of parental woosh. Mr. Wonka's apparent meanness, though temporarily disheartening, is not seen by children as an excuse for Charlie to allow himself to be corrupted. The triumph of Charlie's integrity is doubly sweet to children precisely because Mr. Wonka's actions seem so unfair. Children understand that they all are at the mercy of random adult lunacies, just as arbitrary and senseless.

Children like Dr. Suess books in general, but some more than others. *The Cat in the Hat* is scary to some children. Strangers taking over their lives in the absence of parents is a real fear, although for some reason the same children are not disturbed by Maurice Sendak's *Pierre* and *Where the Wild Things Are,* perhaps because Pierre looks more intrepid than the lion, and the boy in *Where the Wild Things Are* seems in complete control of his nightmare, something we all wish for. The children is Seuss's *Cat in the Hat* appear passive and not in control.

Seuss's *The Five Hundred Hats of Bartholomew Cubbins* is popular with all children. Bartholomew is caught up unwillingly in an adult world of incomprehensible rules which the child breaks without meaning to. The absurdity of Bartholomew's situation—more and more hats increasing in size and gorgeousness right up to the executioner's block, is not any more preposterous than the king's inability to see that Bartholomew is frantically trying to bare his head as the king wishes. The king's wrath when Bartholomew fails to feed the king's vanity is bitterly familiar to children used to placating adult egos.

Bartholomew Cubbins, like other Suess books, is very scarce, and hardly ever turns up in the general stock of used-book shops or at sales, but there are still plenty of Suess books out there, both new and used.

Jean de Brunhoff's "Babar" stories continue to delight children. From his very first appearance in *The Story of Babar* in which Babar witnesses the killing of his mother, goes to Paris where he is befriended by a rich, aristocratic old lady who buys him handsome clothes, then returns to his own country, Babar the elephant entered straight into the hearts of children.

Children cannot get enough of Babar, and Queen Celeste, his charming wife, Zephir the monkey in his rakish blue beret, and the elephant children, Flora, Pom, Alexander, and Arthur in his colorful French sailor suit. They enchant children, and Babar himself shows children that they can grow to be useful and good however difficult their early years. Children have wept for the young Babar and have watched him grow into a wise and kind monarch, a world traveler, scholar and linguist who still takes time to go searching for Father Christmas, so the children in his kingdom can receive toys on Christmas Day like other children.

Babar, though a king, is very reassuring to children. On his travels he leaves his crown at home so he will not be recognized. When three mice in his hotel room offer to take him to Father Christmas, Babar becomes very excited. "How wonderful! What really extraordinary luck! Just give me time to put on my dressing gown, and I'll be with you," he tells them. When the mice show him not the real Father Christmas, but a doll, Babar is not angry or rude to them. This means a lot to children.

The early Babar books in the original French and in English translations are sought by collectors and are very scarce, although they still turn up. Random House still publishes Babar books in both hardcover and paperback, and since children should have new books added to their libraries (a new fresh copy of *Babar's Spanish Lesson*, for example, costs far less than a video game cassette), they can be added for birthday or holiday gifts, or to cheer up a child. Book giving does not really require an occasion, however, and it is better to buy new books a child needs now to grow with, than to wait to find these particular books like the Babar series, second hand.

Children, if they have managed to stay sane until the age of six, enter school with lively, untrammeled intelligence. And what are they given to nourish that intelligence? Textbook readers with only a certain number of words the experts dictate as the number the child can handle, even though the child's spoken vocabulary exceeds the experts' limits by hundreds, sometimes thousands of words.

Reading is taught joylessly, as a "language skill." The child does not read for the thrill of learning what happens to the boy in the space ship, or how people live in an African village, or what makes a tadpole turn into a frog.

Adults joke about the maddeningly boring textbooks children must use, forgetting that children are oppressed by these textbooks and by the system that uses them. There is no point to learning how to read if all that is gained is more "polishing of skills" by swallowing more of these insulting textbooks, and filling up more and more workbooks that are just "make work." Perhaps this is why children love the old school readers, the National Reader, and the old Heath

LESSON XXIV.

thŏr'ōugh ly	mŏnth	drīed	dȳed	ċŭts
shēar'er	shēep	thōṣe	spŭn	dīrt
ŏth'er wīṣe	wōv'en	ċlŏth	wŏŏl	rŭb

SHEEP-SHEARING.

1. Sheep are washed and sheared some time in the month of June. This should be done quite early in the month, before the hot days begin.

From McGuffey's Second Eclectic Reader.

2. It is fine sport for those who look on, but not much fun for the sheep.

3. It is best for the sheep to have the wool taken off; otherwise they would suffer in the summer time.

4. When the time comes for washing the sheep, they are driven to a pond or a little river.

5. Then they are thrown into the water, one at a time. The men who are in the water catch them, and squeeze the wet wool with their hands to get the dirt all out of it.

6. When the wool is thoroughly dried, the sheep are taken to the shearer; and he cuts off the wool with a large pair of shears.

7. It is then dyed, spun, and woven into cloth.

8. In a short time, before the cold winter comes, new wool grows out on the sheep. By the coming of spring there is so much, that it must be cut off again.

Readers, with their plump, rich black print. These old readers are the relics of our own happy apprenticeship in literacy and are still available in used book shops and at sales, particularly those of small town libraries.

Children are drawn to these books because they tell them things they want to know. A group of children in one story will build a kite. The moon will tell what is happening when it appears to grow and shrink; animals and flowers, the wind and the sun tell the young readers how the natural world goes about its business, and the young readers come to know and respect nature, and their place in it.

The advanced textbook readers contain the writings of Emerson, Thoreau, Charles Lamb, Thackeray, Dickens, Poe, Prescott, Hawthorne. The selections include history, exploration and discovery, science and poetry. They are the original works, not cut-up, or "digested." As one ten year old said of the works in his Heath and Butler series readers, "they have meat on them."

The progressive sensibility might recoil from the provincialism and patriotism expressed in some of the selections in these old readers. Some adults may be uncomfortable with the moral and ethical examples that were considered essentials of education in the past. But these old readers introduce children to literature and to a wider knowledge of history and natural science, and they do so cheaply. And children learn to navigate around the shoals of cant and hypocrisy; they do it every day in their own lives.

Odd, obscure books can become children's dog-eared favorites: Prince Ghosh's *Wonders of the Jungle* (D.C. Heath, Boston, 1915), or *The Sea and Its Wonders* by Mary and Elizabeth Kirby (T. Nelson, London, 1871). Adults who question these choices, or disparage or joke about them make children unsure of themselves. Children should feel free to explore the world of books on their own.

When children reach puberty, there is so much going on in their bodies, and in their social development that they will want to read everything their friends read: romances, stories about troubled children, and books that adults may consider inappropriate, such as stories about juvenile delinquents or city street gangs. Children really live in these latter stories. They feel friendship and love for the characters. Again, adults should not probe children for their reasons for reading these books. Children learn from these books what Maria Montessori calls "the cornerstone of education, (that) 'all men are brothers'."

Children should not be victimized by I.Q. scores, and forever denied the great adventure of learning because of a number that purports to measure what is essentially unmeasurable—curiosity, imagination, the capacity for wonder, the thirst to know.

In *Education and Peace* (Henry Regnery, 1972), Maria Montessori writes, "By considering the child as a passive *tabula rasa*, without inner directives, the adult has in fact forced him to bend to the will of his elders and adapt to the conditions of the adult world. The adult has thus repressed the child's sensitive natural inclinations and trampled them underfoot, rousing in him unconquerable instinctive resistances and defenses capable of degenerating into real spiritual illnesses."

The children of parents who do not understand this might be star pupils, always shooting up their hands before the teacher finishes the question. Stuffed like a Christmas goose with facts and garnished with academic lauds, they graduate and are heard from no more. A star pupil of this type is a good little *tabula rasa*, but so jealous is he of his facts and his superiority to his classmates that he has little time to dream, or to imagine anything more satisfying than getting the highest scores. This is sad. For humanity is not propelled forward by high scores achieved in a vacuum.

To pit children one against the other as is done in most classrooms without allowing for differences in temperament, rates of growth, home environment and the effects of unlimited television watching, fosters a system of caste and class that is evident to every child who makes it to high school. But even before this the testers have separated the sheep from the goats, the "winners" from the "losers", and all children suffer from this arbitrary and unnatural separation.

Stephen Jay Gould in his recent book *The Mismeasure of Man* (Norton, 1981) writes, "We pass through this world but once. Few tragedies can be more extensive than the stunting of life, few injustices deeper than the denial of an opportunity to strive, or even to hope, by a limit imposed from without, but falsely identified as lying within."

Adult Reference List for Children's Home Library

James Baldwin, *No Name in the Streets.* Dial Press, 1972.
Stephen Jay Gould, *The Mismeasure of Man.* W.W. Norton Publishers, 1981.
Paul Hazard, *Books, Children, and Men.* The Horn Book, Inc., 1947.
Maria Montessori, *Education and Peace.* Henry Regnery, 1972.
Richard Rodriguez, *Hunger of Memory: The Education of Richard Rodriguez, An Autobiography.* David R. Godine, Publisher, 1982.

Used Book Sales

Book collecting is no longer thought of as a hobby for only the very rich, or as a pastime of scholars. There are as many kinds of collectors as there are books. There is the high-school junior who, in the sixth grade, became enthralled by Scott's fatal expedition to the South Pole, and now owns the nucleus of a valuable polar regions collection.

The most valuable book in his collection cost him five dollars. He has been offered twenty times that figure, although the book is in poor condition. But the book has fine plates that can be sold singly.

A young matron built her collection on the development of psychiatry in America. She had no formal training in the subject and no compelling curiosity about it.

As a student in college she had read Nancy Milford's biography of Zelda Fitzgerald (Harper & Row, 1970). She had been baffled by the medical transcript of Zelda's psychiatric sessions in which the psychiatrist forbade her to write fiction and defined for Zelda the normal role of a loyal wife.

It is difficult for those who have lived within an accepted orthodoxy, whether religious, political, or scientific, to comprehend how peculiar that orthodoxy appears to those for whom it has become a dead letter.

THE FIRST HOUR OF A LARGE USED-BOOK SALE IS NOT FOR THE FAINT OF HEART.

Twenty-five years after the Inquisition, young girls walking along a road telling each other's fortunes might have been astonished or amused by an old peasant woman's fearful warning cries.

The college student felt the same when she read of Zelda's psychiatric experiences. But passing a second-hand bookstore one day, she saw a copy of Harry Stack Sullivan's *Personal Psychopathology* in the ten-cent bin on the sidewalk. She bought it, and around that book she built a respectable collection. This was ten years ago when medical and scientific texts were not a popular specialty. Her collection increases in value yearly.

During our country's bicentennial celebration American history came alive for Americans in cities and small towns. They looked to the past for knowledge of the people and events that had shaped that history. Old books came out of attics and private libraries—old diaries, account books, letters. Historical societies and university libraries opened their doors to ordinary citizens eager for news of the past.

And when the last mock battle was fought on a New England green, and the last staged Indian attack was repulsed in a small prairie town, young and old often were not satisfied to turn back to television to learn who they were and how they came to be here.

Once in a while television will tell us a story that, despite its flaws, has the power to ignite a whole people. Denied a place in American history, black Americans embraced Alex Hailey's *Roots* as a testament to their presence. "Roots," for both black and white Americans, was the starting point for exploring their racial and ethnic memories.

The rise of the feminist movement in the past few decades created the same interest in quickening the voices of the past silenced in man's history, with its rumors of war and celebration of men's deeds.

But where was this past? Was it locked away in a computer accessible only to the expert on information retrieval? How would the expert know what we wanted him to retrieve? Who decided what information we would want to be stored in the first place?

For forty centuries, since the Sumerians first etched into clay the symbols that defined their reality, the names for what grew in the field, the names for what they did and what they felt, the printed word has been mankind's vessel of memory. And for five centuries the book has made our memories portable.

But where does the young black, the housewife in South Dakota, the mechanic in Kezar Falls, Maine, the rancher in New Mexico, the banker in New York, the student, the researcher, go to find the books that hold the memories they need to recall?

They go to the book barns in rural hamlets, or to the used book shops in small towns and large cities. They regularly visit public libraries that sell donated books and library discards. They attend the large used book sales such as the Smith College Club sales, and sales sponsored by churches, hospitals, and other institutions.

They might plan their vacations around the Cyrenius H. Booth Public

Library sale (40 to 50,000 volumes) in Newtown, Connecticut, or the Jesup Memorial Library sale (8 to 12,000 volumes) in Bar Harbor, Maine.

The high-school junior whose specialty is polar regions notifies his lawn-mowing and house-painting customers in early spring of his "away" days.

At the end of April he and his sister, a veterinarian's assistant and a collector of courtesy books, drive her van to Portland, Maine for the annual Armory sale sponsored by the Auxiliary to the Cumberland County Medical Association.

At the sale they find books in their own specialities from 25 cents to one dollar. They also pick up a copy of Richard Wright's *Native Son*, first edition, in pristine dust jacket. They buy a 19th century children's book with fine color plates, a signed Robert Frost first edition, and a 19th century medical textbook on the surgery of the hand. Each book cost 50 cents.

These are not titles the two young people collect; the books are out of their specialties. But with a neighbor they subscribe to *Antiquarian Bookman's Weekly*. Sporadic readings of the want lists and studious reading of the essays contributed by antiquarian dealers, rare book curators, librarians, and collectors educated them on what is being collected outside their specialties.

In June they venture southward to Rhode Island, to the Public Library sale in Westerly (20 to 30,000 books). Joining them on this trip is a neighbor, a young factory worker who builds Friendship sloops from the original plans.

He has accumulated a number of old books on boat building and sailing, all out of print, several very scarce in any condition. These will be the nucleus of a collection on sailing crafts of his region. He and his friends will stop in Bristol to visit the Current Company to see that shop's remarkably fine collection of American Cup racing, and to discuss plans for his collection with Robert Miller, proprietor of Current Company.

The appeal of book collecting to everyone—from very young children, to students, to the mechanic who hang-glides on weekends and has a superb collection of early flight prints and books that he collected on the twenty dollars a month he allowed himself—is that you set your own course, and in most instances, do not need a lot of money. It is immensely satisfying for a twelve year old girl to be an expert on 19th century American etiquette books, all of which were purchased from an allowance of one dollar a week.

Many collectors may not be able to compete with institutional buyers at rare book auctions, but all collectors can attend used-book sales; they can head for the book table at church and community fairs; spare a few minutes to check out titles on the permanent sale table at libraries. Dealers, collectors, and home library builders are always adding to their stock and collections from these sources.

I hope the beginning collector will not scorn the table of old books offered at the small, out of the way libraries; an 1884 edition of Henry James's *A Little Tour in France* will be a welcome addition to a collection centered on 19th century American authors in Europe, even with the book plate of a Vermont hamlet's social library on the pasted-down end paper.

84

New collectors and home library builders should not be discouraged by the presence of dealers at these sales. It is a good sign, for dealers try to attend worthwhile sales.

Dealers can, and very often do, overlook valuable books because of haste or because they are unfamiliar with books outside their own specialties. New dealers may not be aware of new trends in collecting, such as American decorative trade bindings, or books for and about adolescents from the late 19th century through the 1930's, many illustrated by collectible artists. Many dealers have little interest in science fiction so the prices of many sci/fi books have soared in the catalogues of dealers who do specialize in science fiction titles. Yet these titles are not that scarce, and turn up frequently at used-book sales for less than a dollar.

The dedicated volunteers who run these sales are careful in assigning books to their proper category table, but I have found books "out of subject" often enough to encourage me to look through those categories that hold little interest for me.

At a recent sale I found a first edition of Willa Cather's *Not Under Forty* on the Science/Mathematics table, and a later edition of Van Wyck Brooks's *The Confident Years* presuming to transmit a bit of cheery optimism to an aloof Henry Adams's *Democracy*, both misplaced on the Government/Politics table.

Used-book sales are held either on a permanently fixed annual date, around a national or local holiday, or at a time convenient for the dedicated men and women who sponsor and work the sale.

They collect books throughout the year, sometimes driving long distances to pick up donations. They spend hundreds, and on the gigantic sales such as the Mark Twain Library Sale in Redding, Connecticut, thousands of hours inspecting, dusting and separating donations into categories.

Sometimes they give up rooms in their houses to store the books, then days before the sale they haul the books to the sale location, set up the tables, and relinquish their charges.

If the sale site, the armory or community house, is used by other organizations just before the sale, setting it up may have to be done in a matter of hours before the doors open.

Since these sales are held to raise money for aiding financially straitened

85

public libraries, for college scholarships, hospital equipment, and other worthwhile projects, all labor is volunteer.

When I enter a sale and survey the results of this tireless dedication I want to make a bow to the volunteers, but they are much too busy to notice.

There are snack bars at some sales, offering homemade muffins, sandwiches and coffee at reasonable prices—after your books are selected. If sale customers are forgetful and carry food or beverages around the books, they will be reminded by volunteers or other customers that this is not done.

Sometimes libraries will not have strong support organizations. In some small, rural New England towns just getting someone to open the library doors a couple of times a week can be a problem. The library may be a room in the old town hall. Salaries offered are negligible, one or two hundred dollars a year, if anything, and are paid from town trusts or small allocations from town funds voted at town meeting.

Since many of these towns have no broad industrial or commercial tax base, library funding is not considered a top priority. The libraries more often close in winter, or open for only a few hours one evening a week if wood has been provided for the stove.

The used-book sales at these libraries may not offer the number and variety of books available at larger sales, but they often turn up books of interest and even of value.

Many sales do not have a permanent time and place. Make a telephone call or send a stamped, self-addressed postcard a few weeks before the approximate time given, to obtain this information. No answer should be expected by mail if a stamped postcard is not included with your request.

Dealers, collectors, and those building fine home libraries attend these sales. The books are in excellent condition, in all subjects, and the prices range from ten cents to one or two dollars, and are generally reduced more than half in the last hours of the sale.

The larger, older sales may have an appraiser; the appraiser's selections are sold in separate sections, or sold at auction on preview nights. Preview nights are festive occasions, sometimes open to the public for a slight donation, usually two or three dollars. At some preview nights books are sold for double the sale price, and even then the books are bargains and sell quickly.

More young people are turning up at preview nights, students and young married couples intent on establishing good personal libraries cheaply. The beautiful old sets of Dickens, Thackeray, Austen, Trollope, and our own American writers, Hawthorne, Irving, Prescott, Twain, can be picked up at these sales, complete, for anywhere from five to twenty-five dollars. A few years ago it was difficult to give these lovely sets away, except to interior decorators who bought them by the yard, but there is new interest in 19th century authors and the sets they were collected in.

When people say they love books but simply do not have any place to put them, what they are really saying is that those nasty old dust catchers would ruin their decor.

They are unwilling to give shelter to foundlings. But a true book lover will take in an old book even if it does not look especially dapper. The book may have an air about it; in its worn half leather it has a certain insouciance, as if it's been around and can still tell you a few things, as almost every book can, even the awful ones.

The attraction of book collecting has been defined as the lure of the chase. Following are over one hundred used-book sales held throughout the year in New England. Happy hunting!

Used Book Sales
in New England

Connecticut

Cheshire

CHESHIRE PUBLIC LIBRARY. 104 Main Street, Cheshire, CT 06410.

The Cheshire Public Library Association holds an annual sale usually in the early spring at the Library. There are approximately 5000 volumes in all categories plus magazines and records. Cheshire residents donate books and related items so there are few library discards. Main Street is also Rtes. 68 and 70.

Coventry

BOOTH AND DIMOCK MEMORIAL LIBRARY. Coventry, CT 06238. *Tel:* 203/742-7606

The Library's annual sale is held on a Saturday at the beginning of October at the Patriot's Park Dining Hall, Lake Street, Coventry. Lake Street is off Rte. 31, opposite the Post Office. Approximately 3500 books.

Danbury

DANBURY PUBLIC LIBRARY. 170 Main Street, Danbury, CT 06810. *Tel:* 203/797-4505

Friends of the Danbury Public Library hold a three day sale at the Library, usually in the spring. There is a Preview Evening on the first day of the sale when an admission fee of $2.00 is charged. No admission is charged for the remaining days of the sale. The sale includes special books of interest to the collector, current fiction and non-fiction, cookbooks, children's books, and a gratifying selection of "how-to" books for the handyman. The proceeds, as with all library sales, directly benefit the Library and its programs. According to my correspondent Friend, this sale is a chief source of revenue for the organization, and a popular event.

Darien

DARIEN LIBRARY. 35 Leroy Avenue, Darien, CT 06820. *Tel:* 203/655-2568

The book sale is held during Darien's "Sidewalk Sales Days," usually in July, at the Library. The Library is immediately off Exit 11 of the Connecticut Turnpike in Darien. There are approximately 2000 books for sale.

Farmington

THE VILLAGE LIBRARY. 71 Main Street, Farmington, CT 06032. *Tel:* 203/677-1529

Traditionally, the Farmington Library holds its sale on the first weekend of October, with a Preview Night held on Thursday. The sale is always held in the Library on Main Street (Rte. 10) and there are approximately 3500 to 5000 books for sale.

Groton

GROTON PUBLIC LIBRARY. 52 Route 117, Newtown Road, Groton, CT 06340. *Tel:* 203/448-1552

The Friends of the Groton Public Library hold an annual sale at the Library on a Saturday in mid-May from 9 a.m. to 3 p.m. The Library is located on Rte. 117 about one half mile south of exit 88 off I-95. Over 2000 books are available in all categories.

Ledyard

THE LEDYARD LIBRARIES. Box 225, Ledyard, CT 06339

Ledyard Friends of the Libraries conduct an annual sale the first weekend after Labor Day during the Ledyard Fair. Sale location is inside the fair grounds, in the gymnasium of the elementary school. Admission is charged to the fair grounds. Ledyard is in southeastern Connecticut, 10 miles north of I-95 on Rte. 117. Books include fiction, non-fiction, children's, sets, and special items.

Mystic and Noank

MYSTIC AND NOANK LIBRARY. Mystic, CT 06355

Annual sale held first Saturday in June at the Library, 40 Library Street, Mystic. Library Street intersects with Rte. 1 (West Main Street) and High Street at the Union Baptist church. The Library is in the orange brick Victorian structure next to the church. Book sale is held in conjunction with Friends of the Library's "Spring Fling," which includes bake and gourmet food sale, plant sale, children's activities, silent auction, and so on. Time: 10 a.m. to 3 p.m. on the first Saturday, book sale continues inside the Library, during regular hours, for the next two weeks. Approximately 2500 to 3000 books.

New Canaan

DARIEN-NEW CANAAN-NORWALK-WILTON SMITH CLUB SALE. Waveny Mansion, New Canaan, CT 06840

Another great sale. Between 50 and 70 thousand volumes in all categories, all very fine. There is a separate room reserved for rarities. This is an extraordinarily well organized and presented sale. It has been held annually for over twenty years. In 1984, it will be held April 5 through 9. Hours are Thursday and Friday, 9:30 a.m. to 8:30 p.m., Saturday 9:30 to 5:00, Sunday 11:00 a.m. to 5:00, Monday 9:30 to 12:30. Lines form early. At 7:00 a.m. on the first day one hundred numbers are given out to avoid a crush at opening time.

Take exit 37 off the Merritt Parkway, go along South Avenue (Rte. 124) for three miles. Turn left at Waveny Mansion drive.

New Haven

NEW HAVEN COLONY HISTORICAL SOCIETY. 114 Whitney Avenue, New Haven, CT

The Society holds a tag book sale and auction on the last weekend of April. The separate auction items may be previewed on tag sale day, the day before the auction. There are about 7000 books offered at the tag sale.

In 1983 the Society held its first annual sale only day on the last weekend in February with about 10,000 books offered. No definite date has been established for this sale. A Society spokesperson suggests sending a stamped, self-addressed postcard at the end of December for future sale only dates.

Sales and auctions are held at Society headquarters at the above address.

In October the Society hosts an area Antiquarian Booksellers Fair, at which the Society also offers used books for sale.

Newtown

CYRENIUS H. BOOTH LIBRARY. Main Street (just south of flagpole), Newtown, CT 06470

One of the largest used book sales in New England and certainly one of the best. Just about every subject is represented in the 45,000 volumes offered. Many scarce out of print titles and an unusually fine selection of illustrated books from Art through Zoology, e.g., *Icones Farlowianae* by William Farlow, 1929 Harvard University, *Catalogue of the Ironwork of the Paris Exposition* by Henri Martinie, 1925. Great finds in every category. Sale is held on the Labor Day weekend starting on Saturday at 1:00 p.m. As with all the greats, lines start forming hours earlier. Do not despair. I have found rarities in the last hour of great sales and you can too.

Old Lyme

LADIES BENEVOLENT SOCIETY. First Congregational Church, Old Lyme, CT 06371

A White Elephant Sale started around fifty years ago includes a book section of approximately 1000 hardcovers and 1000 paperbacks. Sale is held at Parish House and grounds on the Thursday and Saturday mornings after Fourth of July. The church is at the head of Lyme Street.

PHOEBE GRIFFIN NOYES LIBRARY. 2 Library Lane, Old Lyme, CT 06371

The Library holds an annual book sale, no fixed date, usually in the fall. There is a Preview Night on Friday with books costing twice the marked price. Saturday books are at the marked price and half price last hour on Sunday. The sale is usually held at the Lyme-Old Lyme Middle School. Beginning in June the Library solicits gifts of used books from the community, old and new fiction, non-fiction, art books, cookbooks, children's books, etc., numbering in the thousands. This is a very well organized sale. An unusually large selection of children's books both hardcover and paperback. An interesting selection of rare and sought after out of print titles. The Board of Managers of the library sponsors the sale. The Middle School is in the historic district behind and to the right of the Old Lyme Fire Department.

Oxford

OXFORD PUBLIC LIBRARY. Oxford, CT 06483

The Library holds a sale during National Library Week in April, and a second sale in the fall on Election Day, the first Tuesday in November, along with a community effort bake sale. The Library is located on the ground floor of Oxford's new Stephen B. Church Memorial Town Hall. To reach the parking lot in the rear of the building, one must go past the Library door. The Library is located in the center of Oxford, on Rte. 67, about fifteen miles northwest of New Haven.

Redding

MARK TWAIN LIBRARY. P.O. Box 9, Redding, CT 06875

The annual Book Fair of the Mark Twain Library is held on Labor Day weekend. Traditionally, it opens on Friday afternoon, 2 p.m. to 9 p.m. for a preview sale at which all items are double the marked price. The hours on Saturday, Sunday, and Monday are 9:30 to 5:30. The sale is held at Redding Elementary School on Rte. 107 in Redding Center. Rare books are auctioned on Saturday at noon; catalogue information is available in advance by sending a stamped, self-addressed business size envelope to the Library. This is one of the largest sales in New England with approximately 40,000 books. A great.

Sherman

SHERMAN LIBRARY. Sherman, CT 06784

The annual library sale is held in the summer, usually in July. In 1982 the three day sale offered approximately 3000 books, including many collector items.

Southport

PEQUOT LIBRARY. 720 Pequot Avenue, Southport, CT 06490. *Tel:* 203/259-0346

Pequot Library has been holding annual book sales for over twenty years, usually in mid-summer, on the Library grounds and inside the Library in the auditorium. This is another large, expertly organized sale offering approximately 30,000 books for sale. Southport is located off I-95 at Interchange 19.

Stratford

STRATFORD LIBRARY ASSOCIATION. Stratford, CT 06497

Friends of the Stratford Library sponsor an annual book sale usually on Father's Day weekend. The sale is held at the Library on Main Street, one block east of Exit 32 on the New England Thru-way (I-95). There have been 19th century books of interest to the collector among the approximately 8000 books offered for sale.

Suffield

KENT MEMORIAL LIBRARY. Main Street (Rte. 75), Suffield, CT 06078

The annual Library book sale is held on the weekend after Labor Day in the Library courtyard, inside the Library during inclement weather. The Library is in the center of town. A very creditable 5000 volumes are offered for sale.

Wilton

WILTON LIBRARY ASSOCIATION. 137 Old Ridgefield Road, Wilton, CT 06897

Books are sold on a regular basis. A rare book sale is usually held early in May with occasional rare book auctions. All are held at the Wilton Library.

Maine

Bar Harbor

THE JESUP MEMORIAL LIBRARY. 34 Mt. Desert Street, Rte. 3, Bar Harbor, ME 04609. *Tel:* 207/288-4245

For twelve years many visitors to Maine have been planning their vacations to coincide with this exceptionally fine sale.

Usually held on the third Saturday in August, the sale is conducted inside and outside the Library; Rte. 3 is one of Bar Harbor's main streets.

Offered for sale are old books in fair to excellent condition, both fiction and non-fiction, children's books—old and new, poetry, music (lots of old sheet music), foreign language books, cooking and gardening books, new fiction and non-fiction in hardcover, and books about Maine. There is also a separate room for very special books.

In conjunction with the used book sale there is a large sale of home pre-pared foods, and a luncheon is served on the grounds at the rear of the library. Approximately 8000 books for sale.

Bath

PATTEN FREE LIBRARY. Summer and Washington Streets, Bath, ME 04530. *Tel:* 207/443-5141

Annual book sale held on July 4 from 10:00 a.m. to 4:00 p.m. in the park adja-cent to the Library. There are several thousand books, both hardcover and paperback, priced at 10 and 25 cents.

Boothbay Harbor

BOOTHBAY HARBOR MEMORIAL LIBRARY. Corner Townsend Avenue and Oak Street, Boothbay Harbor, ME 04538. *Tel:* 207/633-3112

The Library owns the house next door in which books are sold from June through September, four or five days a week.

The summer long sale features hardcover fiction and non-fiction, old and out-of-print, children's books, cookbooks, gardening, and books about New England and the sea.

Like the Skidompha Library used-book store in Damariscotta, this library sale is a browser's paradise.

The Library is in the center of town. Oak Street is one way entering town, and Townsend Avenue is one way leaving town. Difficult to miss.

Bristol

BRISTOL AREA LIBRARY. P.O. Pemaquid, ME 04558 (mailing address). Bristol, ME. *Tel:* 207/677-2115

The Junior Friends of the Library have begun sponsoring a Spring Book Sale held in the basement of the Longfellow School in Bristol Mills which is temporary headquarters for the Library. The sale is held at the end of April.

Camden

CAMDEN PUBLIC LIBRARY. Camden, ME 04843. *Tel:* 207/236-3440

The annual book sale is usually held on the second Friday in August at the parish house of the Congregational Church, Free Street entrance, from 9:00 a.m. to 5:00 p.m. A very large, well organized sale.

Casco

CASCO PUBLIC LIBRARY. Casco, ME 04015. *Tel:* 207/627-4541

Casco Public Library holds an annual book sale which usually starts the last week of July and runs through August. The sale is held in the Library, located in the center of Casco Village (Rte. 121) during library hours, which are 9:00 to 4:00 on Wednesday and Friday, 1:00 to 4:00 on Saturday. There are between 2,000 and 3,000 books in the sale.

Castine

WITHERIE MEMORIAL LIBRARY. Castine, ME 04420. *Tel:* 207/326-4375

Friends of the Library sponsor an annual sale on the Saturday following the July 4th weekend at Emerson Hall, beginning at 10:00. Emerson Hall is the town hall and is located on Court Street just off Main Street. Books in all categories are included with a "treasure table" of unusual finds and interesting old books.

Cumberland Center

PRINCE MEMORIAL LIBRARY. Route 9, Cumberland Center, ME 04021. *Tel:* 207/829-3180.

The Library has a sale in the spring, around Memorial Day, in the Congregational Church yard. Another sale is held in mid-August on the Library lawn. There are under 500 books.

Damariscotta

SKIDOMPHA LIBRARY. Damariscotta, ME 04543. *Tel:* 207/563-5513

Housed in an addition to the Library on Main Street is the Skidompha Library Bookshop. Its floor to ceiling shelves are filled with fine old books, and out of print newer books in all categories. Good, well-cared for sets of American and British authors, children's books including old school readers. Entrance is through a charming courtyard. The shop is open in summer only. Since the shop is run by volunteers, the hours vary.

Deer Isle

CHASE EMERSON MEMORIAL LIBRARY. Deer Isle, ME 04627. No telephone in library.

The library holds an annual sale in mid-summer, usually at the Town Hall. There are between 500 and 1,000 volumes.

Kennebunkport

LOUIS T. GRAVES MEMORIAL LIBRARY. Main Street (Rte. 9), Kennebunkport, ME 04046. *Tel:* 207/967-2778

The Library holds an annual sale, usually in early August.

North Bridgton

NORTH BRIDGTON PUBLIC LIBRARY. North Bridgton, ME 04057. No telephone in library.

There is an annual sale at the Library from the first week in July through Labor Day on Saturdays from 10:00 to 4:00 and on Wednesday evenings from 7:00 to 9:00. The Library receives books left over from the April Armory sale in Portland, sponsored by the Auxiliary of the Cumberland County Medical Association. Only very fine books in all categories are accepted for the Armory sale, so those of us who brood about the fine books our spouses forbade us to add to the stacks we bought at the Armory sale can look forward to a reunion with them in North Bridgton. In addition, year round and summer residents contribute books from their private collections and old treasures from their attics. Thousands of books are sold over the summer to collectors, students, and home library builders.

Northeast Harbor

NORTHEAST HARBOR LIBRARY. Northeast Harbor, ME 04662. *Tel:* 207/276-5306

Donations and duplicates are sold continually from a small case in the main foyer of the Library. Approximately 200 books over the year.

North Haven

NORTH HAVEN PUBLIC LIBRARY. North Haven, ME 04853

No annual book sale. Books sold year round at the Library.

Old Orchard Beach

LIBBY MEMORIAL LIBRARY. Staples Street, Old Orchard Beach, ME 04064. *Tel:* 207/934-4351

The Library sale starts about a week after school lets out for the summer and continues through the summer until school is back in session.

Phippsburg

ALBERT F. TOTMAN LIBRARY. Phippsburg, ME 04562. No telephone in library.

The Totman Library sells old books, but not on a regular schedule, or at an organized annual sale. The Library is open only on Saturday in the summer, from 2:00 to 4:00 and in winter from 1:30 to 4:00.

Rangeley

RANGELEY PUBLIC LIBRARY. Rangeley, ME 04970

Books for sale at the library year round. Library sponsors a book section at the annual Blueberry Festival, usually on the third Thursday in August. A small sale.

Rockland

ROCKLAND PUBLIC LIBRARY. Rockland, ME 04841

The annual Library Board Book Sale is usually held at the end of June in the basement of the Library. No information on size of sale.

Rockport

ROCKPORT PUBLIC LIBRARY. Rockport, ME 04856

Rockport Library's annual book sale usually held second week in July, Friday and Saturday 10:00 to 4:00 at the Rockport Elementary School cafeteria near the intersection of Rtes. 90 and 1. No information on number of books.

St. George (Tenants Harbor)

JACKSON MEMORIAL LIBRARY. Tenants Harbor, ME 04860. *Tel:* 207/372-8961

The Library annual sale is usually held in conjunction with a summer bazaar on the second Wednesday in August. It is held at the Ocean View Grange, Martinsville, on Rte. 131 (off Rte. 1 north of Thomaston) from 10:00 to 3:00. About 500 hardcovers and 500 paperbacks, with back issues of magazines such as *Audubon, Yankee, Down East, Country Journal* included in the sale.

Skowhegan

SKOWHEGAN PUBLIC LIBRARY. Skowhegan, ME 04976. *Tel:* 207/474-9072

Skowhegan's annual sale is held during the first week in August.

Southport (Newagen)

SOUTHPORT/NEWAGEN MEMORIAL LIBRARY. Newagen, ME 04552. *Tel:* 207/633-2741

The Library sells books in the library throughout the year, as well as old classical records, mostly 78's.

South Portland

AUXILIARY TO THE CUMBERLAND COUNTY MEDICAL ASSOCIATION. South Portland Armory, 680 Broadway, South Portland, ME 04106

Sale is held on the last weekend in April in the Armory. It is a large sale, more than 25,000 volumes. Not surprisingly, there is a large selection of medical and scientific books, early texts, biographies, journals. There is an excellent selection of history, political biography and memoirs. Good sets in these subjects, e.g., Catton, Churchill. Lots of children's books, some early common school readers and geographies, as well as contemporary books.

There are always classics in sets, Dickens, Hawthorne, Twain. In recent years there have been some very nice sets of Thackeray, Eliot, Austen, and one year an interesting looking set of Edgar Allen Poe's works.

There is good fiction in all categories and a very large selection of "nostalgia" fiction—late nineteenth and mid-twentieth century American novels, most of which seem to have been written by women with two or three surnames —Fannie Brimmer Stoat, Mabel Gardner Monk, Florence Bull Hardy-Davis. Many of these books provide beautiful examples of the art of decorative book binding popular when these novels were published. The artistry evident in the design and execution of these bindings are attracting collectors to this relatively uncrowded specialty.

The South Portland Armory Sale is a great sale.

The Auxiliary quite sensibly recognizes that it is not enough to feed the soul, and so offers tasty lunches and pastries for sale in a section *away* from the books.

Southwest Harbor

SOUTHWEST HARBOR LIBRARY. Main Street, Southwest Harbor, ME 04679

The library sale begins in mid-July and continues throughout the summer, one or two days a week, usually Mondays and Fridays. The Library is located next to the Post Office in the center of town. Books for sale are donations in all categories and a few library discards. There are between 1,500 and 2,000 volumes.

Stonington

STONINGTON PUBLIC LIBRARY. Stonington, ME 04681. No telephone in library.

There is usually a sale in the middle of August. However, books for sale are available at all times in the library.

Massachusetts

Acton

ACTON MEMORIAL LIBRARY. 486 Main Street, Acton, MA 01720. *Tel:* 263-9109

Friends of the Acton Libraries hold a book sale in the spring on the Library lawn. It may be at the end of May or some years as late as the first Saturday in June. The Library is located on Main Street (Rte. 27) in Acton Center. Sale hours are usually 10:00 a.m. to 2:00 p.m. and there are about 8000 volumes.

Auburn

AUBURN FREE PUBLIC LIBRARY. 369 Southbridge Street, Auburn, MA 01501. *Tel:* 617/832-2081

The Friends of the Auburn Library have begun holding book sales to correspond with National Library Week, according to my Friend correspondent. Since this is a new venture the number of books has varied. The sales will be held in the Library, which is next to the Auburn Mall.

Bellingham

BELLINGHAM PUBLIC LIBRARY. Box 46—Common Street, Bellingham, MA 02019. *Tel:* 617/966-1660

The Friends of the Bellingham Library sponsor an annual book sale in September on Bellingham Day. The sale is held at Bellingham High School on Rte. 126.

Belmont

BELMONT PUBLIC LIBRARY. 336 Concord Avenue, P.O. Box 125, Belmont, MA 02178. *Tel:* 617/489-2000

The Belmont Library holds two "Bargains for Bookworms" sales each year, one in the spring and one the first Saturday in December. About two or three thousand books from the Library and a small number of donated books are for sale. The Friends of the Belmont Library also hold a used book sale in the early spring.

Beverly

BEVERLY PUBLIC LIBRARY. 32 Essex Street, Beverly, MA 01915. *Tel:* 617/992-0310

Friends of the Beverly Public Library hold monthly book sales on the first Sunday of each month from September through June, from 1:00 p.m. to 3:00 p.m., at the Library, which is located at the intersection of Rtes. 62 E and 22 S, in Beverly.

Boston

BRANDEIS UNIVERSITY SALE. Commonwealth Armory, 925 Commonwealth Avenue, Boston, MA

The annual Brandeis Boston sale is held sometime in April. It is a large, well organized sale, about 25,000 books arranged by category. An excellent selection here for the collector and the home library builder. This is another great sale due to the hard work of its dedicated volunteers. During the year, there are other Brandeis sales throughout New England, and the country.

To learn the exact date of the Boston sale, and sale dates for other Brandeis sales, you may call the Brandeis Women's National Committee headquarters at 617/647-2194 after March 10th.

Boxford

BOXFORD TOWN LIBRARY. 6 Elm Street, Boxford, MA 01921. *Tel:* 617/887-8022

There is a book sale sponsored by the Friends of the Library every September during the Apple Festival in Boxford. The sale is held on the Library lawn. The number of volumes varies from year to year.

Cambridge

CAMBRIDGE PUBLIC LIBRARY. 449 Broadway, Cambridge, MA 02138. *Tel:* 617/498-9080

The Cambridge Public Library holds a sale of approximately 500 volumes on the last working day of each month. Items for sale are primarily duplicate copies, earlier editions, older reference volumes and unadded donations. The sale is held in the vestibule of the Library.

PARENTS ASSOCIATION OF BUCKINGHAM, BROWNE AND NICHOLS SCHOOL ANNUAL ALMOST EVERYTHING SALE. Buckingham, Browne and Nichols School, Upper School Gymnasium, Cherry Landing Road at Fresh Pond Parkway, Cambridge, MA.

Downstairs a huge rummage sale, upstairs the used book sale of approximately 20,000 volumes. This is one of the best sales—good variety of subjects, sound titles in all fields. New non-fiction titles, some review copies, all mint condition, none costing more than two or three dollars. Excellent foreign language section, travel, photography and art books.

This sale has one of the largest and best selections of children's books on the used book sale circuit. Not only are there lots of children's books but many indicate the presence of the international community of scholars and scientists whose children attend this school. At the 1982 sale I bought for twenty cents, the Hamlyn (London) edition of French Fairy Tales retold by Jan Vladislav, with haunting color illustrations by Czech artist Ota Janecek. The book was printed at the Svoboda press in Czechoslovakia with an English text.

The Almost Everything Sale is usually held at the end of October. A stamped, self-addressed postcard for time to the school development office, Buckingham Place, Cambridge, MA 02138.

The first Saturday in May a Circus Day is held at the Lower School, Buckingham Place, at which children's used books are for sale.

Chatham

ELDREDGE PUBLIC LIBRARY. 568 Main Street, Chatham, MA. *Tel:* 617/945-0274

The Friends of the Eldredge Library hold a sale of used books once a year on the Monday following the 4th of July. The sale is held from 10:00 a.m. to 3:00 p.m. on the Library lawn.

Chelmsford

ADAMS LIBRARY. Boston Road, Chelmsford, MA 01824

Chelmsford Friends of the Library will hold its annual sale on the first weekend after Labor Day, Friday and Saturday 9-9, Sunday 9-3. This is another of the very large sales and one of the best. All books sorted by subject, and in addition to the lovely old sets and good books for the home library and collections, there are always rare and unusually fine items turning up at this sale. The sale is held in a large tent on the library lawn. The library is located in Chelmsford Center, easily reached by Rte. 128 and Rte. 3, or I-93 to I-495.

Chilmark

CHILMARK FREE PUBLIC LIBRARY. P.O. Box 180, Chilmark, MA 02535. *Tel:* 617/645-3360

The Chilmark Library has one book sale a year on the last Thursday and Friday of July. It begins on Thursday at 1 p.m. and goes until 5 p.m. Friday hours are 9 a.m. to 5 p.m.

Concord

CONCORD FREE PUBLIC LIBRARY. 129 Main Street, Concord, MA 01742. *Tel:* 617/369-2309

Friends of the Concord Public Library hold an annual book sale on the 1st or 2nd Saturday in June. The sale takes place on the Library lawn at the intersection of Main Street and Sudbury Road from 10 a.m. to 2 p.m. The sale includes a silent auction of rare or unusual books. Number of books—approximately 10,000.

Edgartown

EDGARTOWN FREE PUBLIC LIBRARY. 58 North Water Street, Edgartown, MA 02539. *Tel:* 617/627-4221

The Edgartown Free Public Library sells library discards and gifts to the library that are not added to its collection, on a year round basis. Hardcovers currently sell for 25 cents, paperbacks for 10 cents. Money earned is placed in the E. D. Thayer Fund for the purchase of new library materials. There are about 1200 volumes on display in the Library where the year round sale is held.

Fitchburg

FITCHBURG PUBLIC LIBRARY. 610 Main Street, Fitchburg, MA 01420. *Tel:* 617/343-3096

The Friends of the Fitchburg Public Library hold an annual sale in conjunction with the closing of Main Street for Old Fashioned Bargain Days. The time is usually on the last Thursday in July and the sale is held at the Library. Approximately 3000 volumes are sold each year.

Hingham

HINGHAM PUBLIC LIBRARY. 66 Leavitt Street, Hingham, MA 02043. *Tel:* 617/749-0907

Library book sales are held once or twice a year. No regular schedule. The big sale is usually held in the fall, October or November. Sale is held in the Whiton Room at the Library on Rte. 228 in center of Hingham. About 5000 books, sometimes more.

Gloucester

SAWYER FREE LIBRARY. 2 Dale Avenue, Gloucester, MA 01930. *Tel:* 617/283-0376

Friends of the Library book sale held in the spring at the Library.

Hudson

HUDSON PUBLIC LIBRARY. Wood Square, Hudson, MA 01749. *Tel:* 617/562-7521

There is an annual book sale held in early June. The Library is located at the intersection of Rtes. 62 and 85, off I-495. An average of 3000 to 4000 books is sold.

Lexington

CARY MEMORIAL LIBRARY. 1874 Massachusetts Avenue, Lexington, MA 02173. *Tel:* 617/862-6288

There is a continuing sale of books, magazines and recordings donated to the Library. The number and quality vary greatly.

Lincoln

LINCOLN PUBLIC LIBRARY. Bedford Road, Lincoln, MA 01773. *Tel:* 617/259-8465

The Lincoln Library sale is usually held on the second Saturday in May. For time and place it is suggested that you call or write beforehand. There are approximately 4000 to 5000 volumes.

Lowell

LOWELL CITY LIBRARY—POLLARD MEMORIAL. 401 Merrimack Street, Lowell, MA 01852. *Tel:* 617/454-8821, ext. 249

Friends of the Library sponsor an annual sale during the third or fourth week in May to coincide with the Annual Lowell Regatta Festival. The sale is held in the Library and the number of volumes varies from year to year.

Lynnfield

LYNNFIELD PUBLIC LIBRARY. 18 Summer Street, Lynnfield, MA 01940. *Tel:* 617/334-5411

The Friends of the Library hold an annual sale in October, usually on the third Saturday.

Medford

MEDFORD PUBLIC LIBRARY. 111 High Street, Medford, MA 02155. *Tel:* 617/395-7950

Medford Library has a used book table offering hardcovers for 25 cents and paperbacks for 10 cents. The table is located near the front entrance. There are larger sales in the spring and fall but no fixed date.

Natick

MORSE INSTITUTE LIBRARY. 14 East Central Street, Natick, MA 01760. *Tel:* 617/653-4252

The Morse Institute Library holds an annual book sale on the first or second Saturday of October on the Library's front lawn, or in the bookmobile garage in inclement weather. The Library is located on Rte. 135 about 1½ miles west of Wellesley College.

On sale are gift books and books withdrawn from the Library's collections. Books are in good condition. Past sales have included very good finds in music scores, histories, biographies, and children's books. Prices range from 5 cents to one dollar. Free coffee and doughnuts are served.

New Bedford

NEW BEDFORD FREE PUBLIC LIBRARY. 613 Pleasant Street, New Bedford, MA 02740. *Tel:* 617/999-6291

There is an annual sale usually held during the month of July at the Library. Number of volumes varies each year but there is a good supply of adult fiction and juvenile material from the Library's collection and a limited number of non-fiction books. Also in plentiful supply are paperbacks and some hardcover books donated by patrons.

Newton

NEWTON FREE LIBRARY. 414 Centre Street, Newton, MA 02158. *Tel:* 617/552-7145

Newton Free Library holds an annual book sale in the spring, usually to begin National Library Week activities in April, beginning on a Friday night and going through Sunday.

The Friends of the Newton Library sponsor a continuing book sale in the main library at 414 Centre Street in Newton. No fixed date; all year round.

Pittsfield

BERKSHIRE ATHENAEUM. 1 Wendell Avenue, Pittsfield, MA 01201. *Tel:* 413/442-1559

The Friends of the Berkshire Athenaeum hold outdoor bookstall sales in front of the Berkshire Athenaeum at the corner of East Street and Wendell Avenue, Pittsfield. Sales are held during July and August on Fridays 11 a.m. to 4 p.m., and Saturdays 10 a.m. to 12:30 p.m. Approximately 2000 books are offered for sale on each sale day from a total stock of over 10,000 volumes.

Rockport

CARNEGIE LIBRARY. 2½ Jewett, Rockport, MA 01966. *Tel:* 617/546-6934

The Friends of the Rockport Library have an annual book sale and my correspondent is quite definite as to time and place. The sale is always held on the second Friday in July between 10 a.m. and 2 p.m. at the Community House on Broadway in the center of Rockport. Books are collected throughout the year and there are usually between 5000 and 10,000 volumes.

Scituate

SCITUATE TOWN LIBRARY. 85 Branch Street, Scituate, MA 02066. *Tel:* 617/545-6700, ext. 249

The Friends of the Library sponsor a book sale as part of Scituate Heritage Days. In 1982 the sale was on August 7th from 10 a.m. to 2 p.m. in the lower level meeting room of the Scituate Town Library. There are approximately 2500 books in all categories. The Library is located on Branch Street near the First Parish Road and Beaver Dam Road intersection at Scituate Center.

South Dartmouth

DARTMOUTH PUBLIC LIBRARY. 732 Dartmouth Street, South Dartmouth, MA 02748.

Library's annual book sale usually held in the spring, at the Library.

Sturbridge

JOSHUA HYDE PUBLIC LIBRARY. Rte. 131 and Maple Street, Sturbridge, MA 01566. *Tel:* 413/347-3735

The Annual Book Sale of the Joshua Hyde Library is held on the second Saturday in August. It takes place on the Library lawn next to the Federated Church and across from Town Hall. The sale opens at 9:30 a.m. and closes at 3 p.m. Wide selection of both fiction and non-fiction, children's, and sets. There are approximately 2000 volumes.

Swampscott

SWAMPSCOTT PUBLIC LIBRARY. 61 Burrill Street, Swampscott, MA 01907. *Tel:* 617/593-8380

The Friends of the Swampscott Library hold an annual sale which lasts two weeks beginning the second Saturday after Labor Day. The sale is held in the auditorium of the Library during regular hours. The Library is located on Burrill Street just off Rte. 129 and across from the police and fire stations. The Friends have been conducting sales since 1969 to benefit the Library. Between 3000 and 4000 books are for sale.

Waltham

WALTHAM PUBLIC LIBRARY. 735 Main Street, Waltham, MA 02154. *Tel:* 617/893-1750

The Waltham Public Library has been conducting annual sales for six years in the Library Lecture Hall, and on the lawn in fine weather. The sale is usually held on the last Saturday in September from 9 a.m. to 4 p.m. What is not sold on sale day is sold in the following week during regular library hours. The sale is sponsored by the Friends of Waltham Library, and these dedicated people collect and sort between 10,000 and 15,000 books for the sale.

Wellesley

WELLESLEY FREE LIBRARY. 530 Washington Street, Wellesley, MA 02181. *Tel:* 617/235-1610

The Friends of the Wellesley Free Libraries hold an annual book sale at the Library in the spring.

Wenham

WENHAM PUBLIC LIBRARY. Main Street (Rte. 1A), Wenham, MA 01984. *Tel:* 617/468-4062

The Friends of the Wenham Public Library sponsor a book sale the first or second Saturday in June from 10 a.m. to 2 p.m. on the Library grounds. There is also a "berry and bake" sale at the same time. Approximate number of books is 1000.

Westborough

WESTBOROUGH PUBLIC LIBRARY. West Main Street (Rte. 30), Westborough, MA 01581. *Tel:* 617/366-2812

The Friends of the Library sponsor two book sales. The first is held on the most convenient weekend adjacent to the Fourth of July, either just preceding or just following. The second sale is held under the same conditions at Columbus Day weekend in October. Both sales are held on Saturday on the front lawn or in the meeting room of the Library. Between 5000 and 10,000 volumes are for sale.

West Falmouth

WEST FALMOUTH LIBRARY, INC. West Falmouth Highway (Rte. 28A), West Falmouth, MA 02574. *Tel:* 617/548-4709

The West Falmouth Library sale is scheduled for the last Saturday and Sunday in June each year at the Library which is opposite the old Quaker Church. Sale times are 10 a.m. to 6 p.m. on Saturday; 1 p.m. to 5 p.m. on Sunday. Between 4000 and 5000 books are for sale.

Westport

FRIENDS MEETING HOUSE. Central Village, Westport, MA 02790

For the past twenty years the Society of Friends of Westport has sponsored a used book sale at the Friends Meeting House. Leave Rte. 88 at the Central Village exit and turn right. In 1982 the sale was on July 10, beginning at 11 a.m. There are usually between 4000 and 6000 books.

New Hampshire

Amherst

AMHERST TOWN LIBRARY. P.O. Box 338, Amherst, NH 03031

Friends of the Library sponsor an annual book and bake sale on the first Saturday of June in the Vestry of the Amherst Congregational Church, Amherst Village. The Friends also sponsor a sale in the fall in conjunction with an Arts and Crafts Fair on the Village Common. The first sale is the larger, offering several thousand volumes.

Atkinson

KIMBALL PUBLIC LIBRARY. Academy Avenue, Atkinson, NH 03811.

The Library sponsors a Blueberry Festival in early August at the Library, located just off Main Street (Rte. 121). Duplicates, discards, and donations.

Canterbury

ELKINS PUBLIC LIBRARY. 7 Center Street, Canterbury, NH 03224.

The annual library sale is held in conjunction with the Canterbury Fair usually on the last Saturday in July. Up to 3000 books donated by patrons are arranged on table on the library lawn. Books sell briskly. The last half hour of the sale leftovers go for a penny each. Even at that late hour there was an 1820 book on the "modern" treatment of insanity, and a first edition of *Mad Grandeur* by Oliver St. John Gogarty, inscribed by him to a friend with a note about the switching of the first and second chapters.

Take exit 18 off I-93.

Center Barnstead

OSCAR FOSS MEMORIAL LIBRARY. Center Barnstead, NH 03225

The annual library sale is usually held on the first Saturday in August in conjunction with the Fire Department auction. It is a small book sale, several hundred books arranged on tables on the Library lawn. Most of the books are donations; I have found very fine sporting books, travel journals (West and Southwest), bird and flower books beautifully illustrated. This sale always has books of interest to the collector and home library builder.

From Rochester take Rte. 202A west to Rte. 126 west to Center Barnstead.

Conway

CONWAY PUBLIC LIBRARY. Box 1200, Conway, NH 03818

Sale usually held mid-summer on the Library lawn, Main Street. More than 3000 library discards and donations from the community are for sale.

Cornish Flat

GEORGE H. STOWELL LIBRARY. School Street, Cornish Flat, NH 03746.

The Library has a book sale every summer, usually in July. Approximately 300 books. Cornish Flat is on Rte. 120 between Lebanon and Claremont.

Derry

DERRY PUBLIC LIBRARY. 62 East Broadway, Derry, NH 03038.

Derry Library does not have an annual sale on a regular basis but does have two or three sales a year as gifts and discards accumulate. Derry's collection is very old and both adult and children's sections are being weeded. The library is right in the center of town, in MacGregor Park.

Dublin

DUBLIN PUBLIC LIBRARY. Box 34, Dublin, NH 03444.

The Dublin Library sells books on a regular basis in the Library.

Durham

DIMOND LIBRARY. University of New Hampshire, Durham, NH 03824.

The University of New Hampshire Library holds a book sale twice a year, spring and fall. The spring sale coincides with National Library Week in April; the fall sale is usually in the third week of October. Sales continue for three days. Titles include science, technology, humanities, general fiction, children's books. Prints and recordings are also for sale. Over 1000 books are offered at each sale.

Francestown

GEORGE HOLMES BIXBY MEMORIAL LIBRARY. Francestown, NH 03043

The Library's annual sale is held in conjunction with the Francestown Labor Day Celebration held on the common. Books are sold in the carriage sheds next to the town hall. Numbers vary from year to year, several hundred up. Some very interesting old books here. The Annual Labor Day Celebration will mark its 67th anniversary in 1983.

Take Rte. 114 from Manchester west to Rte. 13, then Rte. 136 which passes through Francestown.

Hampton

LANE MEMORIAL LIBRARY. Academy Avenue, Hampton, NH 03842.

A sale is held in July or August, no permanent date. It is usually held on the Library lawn, corner of Winnacunnet Road and Academy Avenue. More than 1000 books are offered.

Hanover

FIVE COLLEGE BOOK SALE. Alumni Gym, Dartmouth College Campus.

Mount Holyoke, Simmons, Smith, Vassar, and Wellesley alumnae sponsor this large, well-organized sale to raise scholarship funds for the five colleges. The first sale was held in 1962. There are about 20,000 books arranged on tables by subject. Prices reduced last day of sale. There is a nice selection of new university press books at used book prices. Old single issue periodicals like *Harper's* and *Lippincott's*. I found a mint *Harper's* with a Faulkner short story for ten cents in the last hours of the sale. For the exact date send a stamped, self-addressed postcard to: T. J. Sweet, Rip Road, Hanover, NH 03755.

HOWE LIBRARY. 13 East South Street, Hanover, NH 03755.

The Library has a book sale table year round for discards and gift books that are not added to their collection. To get to the Library, turn east off Main Street at the corner south of the Post Office and go on for one block.

Hookset

HOOKSET PUBLIC LIBRARY. 1367 Hookset Road (Rte. 3), Hookset, NH 03106.

Annual sale held on Columbus Day weekend in October, on Saturday, at the Library. Library discards, donations. Approximately 300 books.

Hopkinton

HOPKINTON VILLAGE LIBRARY. Hopkinton Village, Hopkinton, NH 03301

The Friends of the Hopkinton Village Library hold a sale on every Fourth of July, rain or shine. If the Fourth falls on a Sunday, the sale is held on July 3rd. Sale hours are 10 a.m. to 1 p.m., on the lawn of the Library in the center of Hopkinton Village. Take exit 4 off I-89. There are plant, bake, and refreshment sales as well. There is a large and interesting assortment of books at this sale, fiction and non-fiction, new books, very old, tables of obscure titles and unusual subjects, children's books, first editions, sets, and donations from special, private collections. Rare finds occur from time to time. One year, a local dealer gave an unasked for fifty dollars for a book. Books for sale number in the thousands.

Littleton

LITTLETON PUBLIC LIBRARY. 109 Main Street, Littleton, NH 03561.

The Library holds its annual sale near the middle of August. The Library is located in downtown Littleton. Books are not library discards, but slightly used, and well cared for old books from patrons' collections. Items of interest to collectors turn up, Horatio Alger and Joseph Lincoln most recently. All books are donated specifically for the sale. Time of sale is 10 a.m. to 7 p.m. It has been the custom to have a "bag sale" towards the end of the event, a bag full of books chosen by the buyer for $1.50. Books number between 2000 and 3000.

Marlborough

FROST FREE LIBRARY. P.O. Box 416, Marlborough, NH 03455. *Tel:* 603/876-4479

Friends of the Frost Free Library hold an annual book sale in July, no fixed date since it coincides with Old Home Day festivities, and that date is flexible. It is usually the second or third weekend in July. The sale starts at 9 a.m. on the Library lawn and continues until 3 p.m. or until books are sold. Books, magazines in bundles, and recordings.

Meredith

MEREDITH PUBLIC LIBRARY. RFD #2, Box 29, Meredith, NH 03253

A year round book sale is held in the basement of the Library which is located on Main Street. Friends of the Library hold an outdoor book sale on July 3, or thereabout.

Moultonboro

MOULTONBORO PUBLIC LIBRARY. Moultonboro, NH 03254.

Books are sold on a year round basis in the Library, mostly discards and some donations.

Newport

RICHARDS LIBRARY. 58 North Main Street, Newport, NH 03773.

1983 marks the 28th Annual Library Festival with over 5000 books for sale on the library lawn. Books are arranged by categories on tables with a special table for rare and unusual items. This is a well organized and very rewarding sale. Traditionally the Festival is held on the last weekend in August. 1983 dates and times: Friday, August 26, 9-5, Saturday, August 27, 9-3. Books are reduced to half price at closing hours of sale.

Take Rte. 103 west from I-89, or Rte. 103, 11 east from I-91.

North Conway

NORTH CONWAY PUBLIC LIBRARY. Main Street, North Conway, NH 03860.

Annual sale held in late June at the Library from 10 a.m. to 4 p.m., rain or shine.

Peterborough

PETERBOROUGH TOWN LIBRARY. Main and Concord Streets, Peterborough, NH 03458.

Friends of the Library sponsor a book sale every Columbus Day weekend on Friday and Saturday from 10 a.m. to 5 p.m. The sale is held in the large meeting room of the Library, which is located just down the road from the intersection of Rtes. 101 and 202. Titles include fiction, biography, art, music, history, cookbooks, gardening books, books of science and general health. There is a separate room for dictionaries, texts and encyclopedias, and a separate bookcase for books of interest to collectors. Between 3000 and 4000 books are for sale.

Rochester

ROCHESTER PUBLIC LIBRARY. South Main Street, Rochester, NH 03867.

The Library sells books year round. There are about 1000 to 1500 books, double shelved in all categories, some discards, mostly donations. Good boy and girl series, old natural history books, and many Canadian titles, reflecting the presence in Rochester of a large population of French-Canadian descent. Good browsing here. The Library is between the Congregational Church on the corner and Friendly's Restaurant.

Sanbornville

GAFNEY LIBRARY INCORPORATED. Box 517, Sanbornville/Wakefield, NH 03872.

For the past five years Alden Young, recipient of the 1982 Lovell Union Grange —Wakefield Good Citizen Award, has collected books all winter from local and seasonal residents. These books and library discards in good condition make up the annual sale held on the library lawn on the Saturday of the Fourth of July weekend. There are 1000 to 1500 books including lots of old children's books, clean and tightly bound, many late nineteenth century, nicely illustrated, old school readers, "courtesy" books, mid- to late-nineteenth century school geographies. Good American fiction is represented, some first editions, Edith Wharton, Miss Cather; one year I picked up *The Man Who Knew Coolidge* by Sinclair Lewis, not for a collection, but because I had never seen it before.

Sometimes used book sales vary in their variety and depth from year to year, but the Gafney sale, though small, is consistently rewarding. Mr. Young casts a

discriminating net and the books are always of high quality and special interest. This sale is never crowded. Take Rte. 16 north to Rte. 153 toward Sanbornville and Wakefield.

Wolfeboro

HUGGINS HOSPITAL STREET FAIR. On the grounds of Brewster Academy, Wolfeboro.

1983 marks the 46th anniversary of this Fair. The book sale is held in a large tent, about ten to fifteen thousand books. There seem to be more of them every year, and more book buyers lining up for the 10 a.m. opening of the Fair. The Fair is held on the first Friday and Saturday in August. Books arranged by category; some very nice children's books, *Twelve Times One*, N.Y., Worthington, 1888 with lovely color illustrations by Mary A. Lathbury, two Alger titles from the Ragged Dick Series, *Ben the Luggage Boy, Rufus and Rose*, Boston, Loring, 1870. These were picked up in the last hours of the sale, along with the 1930 Cape edition of Kay Boyle's *Wedding Day and Other Stories*.

I judge a sale by what is available at the end of it. It is false to assume that the really worthwhile titles will be gone after the first crush of determined looking dealers and collectors. Dealers may be looking for specific customer wants; collectors for their own subjects. In any case, there are always fine books in all subjects, including very nice sets of an author's collected works, for those building a home library. Take Rte. 11 to Alton then Rte. 28 to Wolfeboro. Brewster Academy is on the left as you enter town.

WOLFEBORO PUBLIC LIBRARY. Box 710, Wolfeboro, NH 03894

Friends of the Library hold an annual sale, usually in late June. The Library is located on South Main Street (Rte. 28), about half a mile south of town, and next to the police/fire station. Library gifts and private donations. Approximately 1200 books.

Rhode Island

Block Island

URIAH B. DODGE MEMORIAL. Island Free Library, Block Island, RI 02807.

In addition to selling books year round, the Library has an annual sale which is always held during the last two weeks of August, through Labor Day. At the annual sale there are between 800 and 1000 books.

While on the Island you may wish to visit Rodman's Hollow, a glacial phenomenon affording an unusual ocean view. The Hollow is home to the small-mouth Block Island meadow vole (genus Microtus), kin to Mr. Rat of *Wind in the Willows*. Come to think of it, the Hollow is the only known home in the United States for this solitary rodent.

Charlestown

CROSS MILLS PUBLIC LIBRARY. Old Post Road, Charlestown, RI 02813

Library's annual sale usually held on the third Saturday in July at the Library, outside in fine weather.

Cranston

WILLIAM H. HALL FREE LIBRARY. 1825 Broad Street, Cranston, RI 02905.

The Library sponsors sales in the spring and fall, but no fixed date.

Gloucester

HARMONY PUBLIC LIBRARY. Located at Adah S. Hawkins Bldg., Putnam Pike, Harmony, RI 02829.

The annual sale is held in the spring at the end of May or the first week in June. Approximately 2000 books for sale.

Lincoln

LINCOLN PUBLIC LIBRARY. Old River Road, Lincoln, RI 02865.

Friends of the Library hold an annual sale in early June along with a Friends sponsored Flea Market and Fair in the meeting room of the Library. Between 2000 and 3000 books are for sale, donations from patrons.

Newport

NEWPORT PUBLIC LIBRARY. Aquidneck Park, Newport, RI 02840. *Tel:* 401/847-8720

In conjunction with the Christmas in Newport festivities, the annual used book sale is held on the first three days of the second week in December. The sale is held in the King Room, downstairs in the library. There are no library discards at this sale; books offered are donations from Newport patrons' collections. Good out-of-print books, children's books—early and contemporary, books on art, hardcover fiction and non-fiction, nicely bound sets of 19th century authors. There are between 5000 and 10,000 books for sale.

While in Newport you may wish to visit the Redwood Library, the oldest library building (1748) in continuous use in America.

North Scituate

NORTH SCITUATE PUBLIC LIBRARY. Greenville Road, North Scituate, RI 02857.

There is an annual three day sale during the Scituate Art Festival held every year on Saturday, Sunday, and Monday of the Columbus Day weekend in October. The sale is held at the Library from 11 a.m. to 5 p.m. The Library is located on Rte. 116 between Rtes. 6 and 101. Over 2000 books are for sale.

Providence

PROVIDENCE PUBLIC LIBRARY. 150 Empire Street, Providence, RI 02903.

Providence Library sells books on a year round basis at its central location, 150 Empire Street, and at its eight branches. Books for sale are discards and gifts from patrons.

Warwick

WARWICK PUBLIC LIBRARY. 600 Sandy Lane, Warwick, RI 02886.

The Library holds its annual sale on the first Saturday of October on the rear grounds of the Library. Approximately 2000 books are for sale.

Westerly

WESTERLY PUBLIC LIBRARY. Broad Street, Westerly, RI 02891. *Tel:* 401/596-2877.

The Friends of the Library hold an annual sale, usually during the first or second week in June. The sale has been held at the local armory on Railroad Avenue, Westerly, but after 1982 it would be wise to contact the Library in advance about the location. (Always enclose a stamped, self-addressed envelope when requesting information about book sales.)

The Westerly Library sale is one of the largest used book sales in New England, and the offerings are superior. A signed Robert Frost, first edition, the first edition of Nabokov's *Lolita* (2 v., paperback, published in Paris), several Lovecraft first editions, are some of the "great finds" that have been reported by happy purchasers. Average hardcover price at the 1981 sale was fifty cents. Prices are reduced for the last half day of the two-day sale.

Magazines, postcards, children's games, phonograph records and other related items are also available. Luncheon is served on the premises. Between 20,000 and 30,000 books are for sale. An exceptionally well organized sale; very fine titles.

Vermont

Arlington

MARTHA CANFIELD MEMORIAL FREE LIBRARY, INC. Arlington, VT 05250. *Tel:* 802/375-6153

Books have lives of their own that transcend the collector's term for their prior ownership, their provenance. Books, like people, are loved, hated, ignored, worshipped, despised and persecuted. Books travel; frontiers do not exist for them. They confound despots who hunt them down. Out of the whirlwind of our wars and diasporas, they come back to us, and we greet them with astonished joy.

Gerald Raftery, former librarian of this library and now president of its board of directors, told of such a reunion in an article he wrote for *Vermont Life* magazine (Summer 1981) about this library's annual sale.

An elderly German looking over the display of foreign language books, "picked up a five volume edition of Schiller's works identical to the one he abandoned in his library when he fled Hitler's regime."

In the same article, Mr. Raftery pays tribute to the founder of the book sale, the late James McCabe, postmaster and library board member. Mr. McCabe gathered books from friends and neighbors all one winter, and "on the day of the Arlington Street Fair, he hauled his accumulation into town on his hay rack."

Since that day, twenty-six years ago, close to a quarter of a million books, magazines and records have been sold and given away.

This is considered the largest used book sale in Vermont and is held from mid-June to mid-October, Friday and Saturday, 10 a.m. to 5 p.m., Sunday, 1-5, on the Library lawn, weather permitting.

Barre

ALDRICH PUBLIC LIBRARY. Washington Street, P.O. Box 453, Barre, VT 05641. *Tel:* 802/746-7550.

Aldrich has three large annual book sales—in the spring, in mid-July and in late September. There is also a small year round sale in the Libary, a yellow brick, Carnegie library with white pillars.

Bennington

BENNINGTON FREE LIBRARY. 101 Silver Street, Bennington, VT 05201. *Tel:* 802/442-9051

The Friends of the Bennington Free Library sponsor an annual book sale during October. The sale is held in the social room of the Library and there are usually about 2000 books.

Brandon

BRANDON FREE PUBLIC LIBRARY. Brandon, VT 05733. *Tel:* 802/247-8230

Brandon has books for sale year round in the Library cellar.

Brattleboro

BROOKS MEMORIAL LIBRARY. 224 Main Street, Brattleboro, VT 05301. *Tel:* 802/254-5290

Brooks Memorial does not presently have a large, annual sale, but they do have books for sale, discards and donations, year round in the Library.

AAUW BOOK SALE. Centre Congregational Church, Brattleboro, VT 05301.

The Brattleboro Branch of the American Association of University Women holds an annual book sale for the benefit of the scholarship fund. The fund provides scholarships for local graduating high school seniors planning to matriculate in a four year college. It also assists mature women who are resuming their studies.

Sale is usually held the third week in July, Thursday, Friday and Saturday, to correspond with a large, local art show on Saturday of that week.

An average of 10,000 books are arranged in many different categories. There are books about New England, and books by New Englanders. A separate table holds special treasures of interest to the collector (a fine first edition of W. B. Yeats' *The Tower*, one year).

Bristol

LAWRENCE MEMORIAL LIBRARY. 40 North Street, Bristol, VT 05443. *Tel:* 453-2366.

The Lawrence Memorial Library sells donations and discarded library books throughout the year. They have a large collection of old magazines such as *Sports Afield* and *Popular Mechanics*.

Chester Depot

CHESTER REVIEW CLUB SALE. Stone Church, Rte. 103, Chester Depot, VT

The Chester Review Club was started nearly a century ago as a reading club and has evolved over the years into a community organization that raises funds for scholarships, school and hospital equipment, the Visiting Nurses Association and other worthwhile community projects.

For over ten years the club has sponsored a used book sale on Columbus Day weekend. The sale is from Friday to Monday from 9 a.m. to 5 p.m., except Sunday, 1 p.m. to 5 p.m.

The sale is held in the lower level of the Stone Church. There are over 10,000 books, donated by local residents.

Take exit 7 from I-91 at Springfield, Vermont; Rte. 11 to Chester, then Rte. 103 to Chester Depot.

Essex Junction

BROWNELL LIBRARY. Box 240, Essex Junction, VT 05452. *Tel:* 802/878-2171

Brownell Library has a continuing sale six days a week. During July the Library is closed on Saturdays.

Killington

SHERBURNE MEMORIAL LIBRARY. Box 73, Killington, VT 05751. *Tel:* 802/422-9765

There is an ongoing book sale in the Library, located on River Road in Killington. May through October book sales are held every Saturday from 10 a.m. to 2 p.m. on the library lawn. River Road is located two miles east of Killington Access Road: the library is one mile down River Road. There are approximately six hundred volumes for sale.

Manchester

MARK SKINNER LIBRARY. Manchester, VT 05254. *Tel:* 802/362-2607

The annual book sale of the Mark Skinner Library is held in August. There are more than 1000 books, the majority contributed by friends of the library.

Montpelier

KELLOGG-HUBBARD LIBRARY. 135 Main Street, Montpelier, VT 05602. *Tel:* 802/223-3338

It is called the "Fifth of July Book Sale" and is held on that date or the next work day following the 5th, and goes on for several days. It is held at the Library and there are approximately 2000 volumes.

Morrisville

MORRISTOWN CENTENNIAL LIBRARY ASSOCIATION. Box 727, Morrisville, VT 05661. *Tel:* 802/888-3853

Held in the library in Morrisville, the "Bastille Day" sale is on July 13 and 14. There are approximately 1000 titles, some very old.

Northfield

BROWN PUBLIC LIBRARY. Main Street, Northfield, VT 05663. *Tel:* 802/485-4621

Brown Library's annual book sale is held on Labor Day. Books are library culls and donations from townspeople. The book sale is part of a gala Labor Day festival. There is a parade, live entertainment, quilt show, flea market, "rides," etc. Northfield is also the home of Norwich University.

Plainfield

CUTLER MEMORIAL LIBRARY. High Street, Plainfield, VT 05667. *Tel:* 802/454-8504

It is the custom at Cutler Memorial to hold two sales a year, one during the first week in June, and the other on Wednesday of Fall Foliage Week, which comes at the end of September or the first week of October. The sales are held at the Library and the number of volumes varies, usually several hundred.

Peacham

PEACHAM LIBRARY. Peacham, VT 05862. *Tel:* 802/592-3216.

Fall in New England is a very busy time—getting the last of the hay in, getting a case of nerves because the ten cords of wood worked up over summer may

not get you through the winter, gathering in and preserving the last of the garden's yield, and preparing for the Fall Foliage festivals.

These festivals are held to make visitors to New England feel more at home but also to give New Englanders an excuse to stop thinking about the awfulness of winter for a few days, or even one day.

The Peacham Library holds its annual book sale in the fall. Frances B. Randall, Librarian, writes: "It is held in September, usually on the last Thursday of the month. This can vary because it is held in conjunction with an area Fall Foliage celebration which gives the surrounding towns one day during that week to emphasize their own particular town. Books left over are sold for several days after Peacham's Day.

"The sale is held here at the Library which is in the center of this small Vermont village. From the south, leave I-91 at Barnet, exit 18, and follow the blacktop north. From the west follow Rte. 2 through St. Johnsbury to Danville then take the blacktop south to Peacham.

"There are approximately 1000 to 1500 books for sale. These books come from our own weeding, from people who are moving, cleaning house or are just generous."

Poultney

POULTNEY PUBLIC LIBRARY. Main Street, Poultney, VT 05764. *Tel:* 802/287-5556.

The Poultney Library holds an annual book sale during the summer, but with no fixed date. Books offered are library discards and donations from collections of library patrons.

Pownal

SOLOMON WRIGHT LIBRARY. Pownal, VT 05261. *Tel:* 802/823-5400

Solomon Wright Library has books for sale at all times. Not many, since it is a very small library.

Proctor

PROCTOR FREE LIBRARY. 4 Main Street, Proctor, VT 05765. *Tel:* 802/459-2946

Proctor Free Library holds book sales in the fall of the year, but not every year, since they must wait until enough books are accumulated. The sale is held in the library. There are from 2500 to 3000 books in addition to magazines, records and old sheet music.

Quechee

QUECHEE LIBRARY ASSOCIATION. Box 105, Quechee, VT 05059.

The Library Association sponsors an annual book sale to coincide with the Quechee Chamber of Commerce Balloon Festival held at the end of June. Included in the sale are about 1000 to 1200 books.

Reading

READING PUBLIC LIBRARY. Reading, VT 05062. *Tel:* 802/484-5588

There is usually one annual sale, in the summer or on Labor Day weekend. Local people donate boxes of books and there are library discards. In 1981 there were about 300 books for sale at 10 and 25 cents. The library is located on Rte. 106 in the Village of Felchville, town of Reading.

Rutland

RUTLAND FREE LIBRARY. Court Street, Rutland, VT 05701. *Tel:* 802/733-6880

Sales are held only when enough gifts, discards, etc., accumulate to warrant a sale, not annually. When sales are held it is usually in August in the basement of the library.

St. Johnsbury

ST. JOHNSBURY ATHENAEUM. 30 Main Street, St. Johnsbury, VT 05819. *Tel:* 802/748-8291

The Athenaeum holds two sales a year, one during National Library Week in April, the second in late September. Each sale is made up of approximately 2000 volumes—discards and donations from the collections of Athenaeum patrons.

Shelburne

PIERSON LIBRARY. Shelburne, VT 05482. *Tel:* 802/985-2040.

Friends of the Pierson Library hold an annual sale the Saturday before Memorial Day weekend. The sale takes place at the Shelburne Town Hall on Rte. 7, five miles south of Burlington. Number of books varies but usually a few thousand, four thousand one year. Sealed bids for collectors' items are submitted at the Saturday opening time of 10 a.m., and bids are opened at noon. The sale was started ten years ago and draws customers from long distances.

South Burlington

COMMUNITY LIBRARY. 550 Dorset Street, South Burlington, VT 05401

Annual sale is usually held on Palm Sunday morning, 8 a.m. to 1 p.m., at the South Burlington High School cafeteria, same address. Sale held in conjunc-

tion with a pancake breakfast. Exit 14E from I-89, right on Dorset at Howard Johnson's. School is half a mile on left.

Windsor

WINDSOR PUBLIC LIBRARY. 43 State Street, Windsor, VT 05089. *Tel:* 802/674-2556

The Windsor Library has an annual sale in mid-August at the Library. It is not, at present, offering much more than library discards.

Winooski

WINOOSKI MEMORIAL LIBRARY. 19 East Spring Street, Winooski, VT 05404. *Tel:* 802/655-0401

Two sales held each year. The first is held during the last day, Saturday, of National Library Week. The second sale is held on the last Saturday in September.

Woodstock

NORMAN WILLIAMS PUBLIC LIBRARY. 10 The Green, Woodstock, VT 05091. *Tel:* 802/457-2295

An annual book sale is held on the library porch and lawn on July 14, from 10 a.m. to 9 p.m. There are new and used books for sale and also some rare children's and adults' books. There are over 2000 books for sale.

Used Booksellers

John P. Dessauer, in *Book Publishing: What It Is, What It Does* (R. R. Bowker), discusses new-book retail stores and concludes that "the real reason why so many book shops incur the wrath of true book buyers and have long ago lost their patronage is that their shelves hold so little attraction for the browser . . . no variety, no depth, no discrimination, no appreciation for the world of books."

Many publishers now rely on their advertising and sales departments to advise what books should be written and published. Much of the stock in new-book outlets has been market-tested just as any other consumer product is, from toothpaste to dog food.

Marketing experts become more important in publishing than literate, discerning editors. Why take a chance on a young writer's first novel, or on good translations of foreign writers? Who cares that they may have permanent value? They don't sell as fast as the autobiography of a hand-puppet.

The marketing experts know that our souls are parched for more and more books on how to cook, and diet and exercise books that show us how to punish ourselves for eating what we cook. The experts give us more books on Zen jogging, transcendental tennis, books that tell us how to floss, how to dress, how to make money, tofu pizza, love, how to be a winner all the time, because that is what our lives are about. Isn't it?

Recently, a French priest who had spent most of his life as a missionary in Africa visited America for the first time. He wanted to visit a bookstore. The only bookstore near the town where he was staying was a chain outlet in a mall on the highway. His host, familiar with European bookstores, knew what the priest expected—a bookstore for people who read. He tried to persuade his guest to wait until they drove in the city the next day, where he knew an independent bookseller whose stock was more varied. But his guest insisted. In the book chain's slot in the mall the priest went from shelf to shelf, from table to table, first bewildered, then dismayed. "But where are the books?" he asked.

The enormous cookbook and dieting sections enthralled him. He waved at a stack of exercise books with the smiling author flashing her fashionably scaphoid abdomen from the cover. His reactions:

"Can you imagine how this must impress students from Africa, Asia, your own neighbors in Latin America? Many are intimately acquainted with famine and brutal toil. These students will be the leaders of their countries someday. How can they take your people seriously, heed your words?

"Your pathological absorption with self is so pervasive it overwhelms what is good in America. Your television, movies, and all these cooking and dieting, feeling and looking good books show what is important to you—your neuroses and your derrieres.

"Your culture seems like that of a spoiled child, like little Inger in the fairy tale who walks on bread to keep from soiling her slippers."

Worthwhile books are being published, even by the much-maligned conglomerate-owned publishers, but in the battle for shelf space in the chains, these books are lost in the blizzard of non-books, the "blockbusters" and "package deals."

There have always been different levels of literary taste and publishers tried to satisfy them. But in the present state of mass-market publishing and distribution, where the tail too frequently wags the dog, only one level is being met consistently, dominating bookstore shelves, and that level is not very high.

The stock in a used-book shop has not been market tested by "bottom-line" experts. The books in these shops have been time-tested. They have endured over time because they speak in their own individual voices, and they address us, each one of us, singly. Their words echo in our hearts and souls and become part of us. We return to these books again and again for they sustain our humanity.

In a used-book shop we always feel quiet exhilaration, the excitement of being in the presence of real books, all kinds of books. They whisper and call to us; they can tell us how to grow small fruits and show us the results of their lessons in exquisite steel engraved plates. They make us understand why "revenge is a kind of wild justice," and how the image of a weeping woman at a railroad crossing gate can uphold us in our season of hell.

In the chain and cut-rate outlets, if you ask for a "non-hyped" book published six months ago, you may be told, as a customer in a local chain outlet was recently told, "We don't carry old stuff. We don't carry things people don't buy. We don't need to. We carry plenty of stuff people buy."

Traditionally, books have not been "stuff people buy," print knick-knacks to fill up the blank walls of people's minds, junk to feed the vanity of up-to-date customers, or to give a quick fix to impoverished imaginations.

Perhaps customers in the chain outlets and the recent phenomenon, the cut-rate outlets where books lie about in cartons and stacks on bare, dirty floors, sense that this "stuff" exploits their genuine desire to read real books. They eat and drink around this "stuff," smearing pages with ice cream and spilled beverages; they kick open cartons of "stuff" on the floor and tread on the contents; fling the latest "stuff" down on the counter, as if they know that it is junk.

The independent new-book retailer must compete with the chains and cut-rate outlets by stocking best-sellers, cookbooks, and so on. Many independents try to include sound titles that will be of interest to the serious readers, the "cultural minority" that traditionally has been the backbone of the trade. Yet the

independents must compete at a disadvantage, for many publishers give the independents smaller discounts than those given to the chains and cut-rates.

Because they consider bookselling a profession, most independents try to offer the traditional services to their customers, services the chains cannot gear down to, and the cut-rate, "books on the floor" outlets disdain.

The independent booksellers try to find out-of-print books; they will special order a recent title even though they know that the book will probably be on the chain outlets' remainder tables by the time (sometimes months later) the special order arrives from the publisher, at the regular price.

Many independent booksellers have begun stocking out-of-print titles in separate sections of their shops and advertising their customers' wants in *Bookman's Weekly*. *Bookman's* puts independent booksellers in touch with thousands of dealers, scouts, and collectors who are able to locate out-of-print and unobtainable recent titles.

In this way the independents can get the wanted books to their customers faster (two to three weeks, average) with fewer bookkeeping costs, and since the booksellers are free to set their own prices, the margin for profit can be much greater than that for this month's "blockbuster."

For the harried independent there is also the bliss of knowing that the very fine second edition of *Death Comes for the Archbishop* bought, still in its pristine dust jacket, from a used-book dealer for three dollars and sold to a customer for seven, will not turn up next week on the chains' remainder tables for two.

The mass market system of book distribution in this country is a nightmare that even those involved in it cannot fully fathom. A book with a small first printing is easily lost in the torrent of books published annually. Books still being sold at list price at one bookstore can sometimes be found on remainder tables in a store down the street for a fraction of the list price.

The number crunching that publishers' accountants do to determine what books will be dropped from publishers' lists does not reflect the reality of how and why real books sell. For example, Russell Hoban's *Riddley Walker* (Simon & Schuster, 1981) was practically unobtainable at bookstores on the day it was nominated for a National Book Award. Within a very short time after its publication it was scuttled off to the remainder tables. Interest in this remarkable book was growing by word of mouth at the same time the book was vanishing from most bookshops. *Riddley* was later issued in paperback, but the original hardcover is being sought by used-book dealers as it is now quite scarce.

What of other books that deserve an audience and need the time the number crunchers refuse to give them? It is the antiquarian and used-book dealers who will save many of these books as they saved the works of Jane Austen—works unread for almost one hundred years—and the works of Melville, Thoreau, and others who were dismissed in their time by critics and academics.

Heading the list of a town or city's cultural attractions should be its used-book shops, for it is their presence that marks a truly civilized community. These bookshops are opening all over the country but in no area are they as numerous and with a wider stock selection than in New England.

Like collectors, used-book dealers span the spectrum of age and of social and economic class. But they all share one purpose: to unite books with those who seek them. Dealers may be retired, successful businessmen, or military officers, whose collections of Emerson, or of Victorian hunting books became the foundations of their stock in trade. The used-bookseller may be a young man who found himself unemployed and owning only an old car and a carton of old comic books. The comic books turned out to be the basis of a five room shop specializing in children's books and children's periodicals going back nearly two centuries; and, of course, old comic books.

An ex-school teacher, now a state senator, moves his growing collection of early American political broadsides and pamphlets out of his house to a vacant shop down the street.

A woman moves the research material for her uncompleted thesis on women and the winning of the West to a room in a remodeled bank building, where a wood fire in winter and a Casablanca fan in summer provide a pleasant climate for her customers.

Less than two years ago, older, long-established dealers lamented the decline of their numbers as more shops closed in city neighborhoods demolished by urban renewal. The Corn Hill section of Boston, a famous center of the antiquarian book trade, vanished as a distinctive setting for the trade, as did the Brick Row section of New Haven. Shops in the Brick Row section had been the schools for learning about book collecting for generations of Yale men. But Yale men—and Yale women—continue the Brick Row tradition at Whitlock's, and at the ten year old Bryn Mawr Book Sale shop, or, by appointment, at the William Reese Company. They are joined by faculty and visiting scholars searching for rare books for private or institutional collections, or for long out-of-print books that are necessary for research that is vital for the preservation and transmission of knowledge.

Even recently published books that have been shoved off retail book outlet shelves because they did not sell fast enough for the number crunchers are sought in used-book shops. The proprietors pick up remaindered titles; from their own knowledge and experience and from conversations with customers, they know what will be sought long after the blockbuster that pushed these remaindered titles aside have been forgotten.

Shops listed in this book's directory were drawn from regional and local dealer lists and from city directories. Each shop was contacted requesting permission to list it in a guide for beginners. Only those who responded were listed.

However, this does not mean that shops not listed do not welcome beginners. Despite several mailings and numerous telephone calls, some very fine shops, long established and newly opened, were overlooked inadvertently. We hope to include these shops in future editions.

Make a practice of stopping at used-book shops to browse. You will soon learn which shops regularly add to their shelves and replenish their sale bins.

Shops that specialize in subjects outside your specialty usually carry a general stock in which you might find just what you need. All good used-book shops are like Christopher Morley's *Haunted Bookshop*; they "have what you want, though you may not know you want it." Buy a book, or several. The prices are, in general, very low, under a dollar in many cases, and though scarce out-of-print titles are usually more, they are often lower than this week's paperback romance.

When we spend more than twenty minutes in a gift shop we feel compelled to buy something, if not by the stares of the salesclerks, then by the impulse to prove that we are not shoplifters or impoverished, or unappreciative of the true beauty of the corkscrew owl. But in a used-book shop we feel no need to purchase anything, even an old geography from the ten-cent bin that would delight an adventurous child. We wander in the stacks of books taking down a volume we recognize from childhood, reading in it for a while and then moving on to another shelf where we take down a book on the French Impressionists, nourishment for color-hungry eyes in a northern winter.

We can spend an intensely pleasurable afternoon doing this and leave the shop without buying anything; we may even add insult to injury by telling the proprietor how lucky he or she is to be surrounded by books all day.

Short of charging admission (not a bad idea considering the enjoyment provided), there is only one way to keep these threatened bookshops alive, and that is to buy a book, just one book, every time we use them to satisfy our weary souls.

To spend hours with thousands of books and then state that we can't find anything we "need" or can "use" is rank silliness. We don't need or use books so much as they need and use us. They need us to live; they use us to transmit what we need to know, and many of them will be lost to us if we do not support the shops that keep them alive for us.

Used Booksellers
in New England

Connecticut

Bethany

WHITLOCK FARM BOOKSELLERS. Sperry Rd., Bethany, CT 06525. *Tel:* 203/393-1240. *Proprs:* Gilbert and Everett Whitlock. *Hours:* All year, open every day except Monday.

You must put Whitlock Farm on your book itinerary. It is probably the largest bookshop in New England with two barns full of thoughtfully selected books arranged for fruitful browsing.

The stock of Americana and other subjects from A to Z as well as maps and prints from every period and place, is always changing.

Whitlock Farm is a perfect place to introduce your children to the joys of building their own library (remember, it's *their* library) or starting their own collections.

You can picnic on the grounds, walk in the woods, and contemplate the universe of books the Whitlocks have gathered up for you.

Take Rte. 69 four miles north of Wilbur Cross Pkwy. and watch for the sign on your left.

Branford

BRANFORD RARE BOOKS AND ART GALLERY. 221 Montowese, Branford, CT 06405. *Tel:* 203/488-5882. *Prop:* John R. Elliott. *Hours:* Open all year, Tuesday thru Saturday, 10:00 to 5:00, Sunday, 1:00 to 5:00.

Some knowledge and a real interest in the specialties here would increase the beginner's enjoyment of this shop.

Branford's specializes in the more traditional collecting areas of cartography, voyages, pre-1900 travel, Americana and fine arts. The nature of its stock makes this shop ideal for the serious beginner who may wish to start a respectable collection in any of these subject areas and is now prepared to enhance his collection with the guidance of Mr. Elliott and the possible acquisition of items from his unusually fine stock.

Located on the Branford Green, or Common.

Colebrook

COLEBROOK BOOK BARN. Rte. 183, Colebrook, CT 06021. *Tel:* 203/379-3185. *Prop:* Robert Seymour. *Hours:* April-October by appointment only.

This shop carries a general stock of used, out of print and rare books.

Directions given with appointment.

Cos Cob (Greenwich)

THE BOOK BLOCK. 8 Loughlin Ave., Cos Cob (Greenwich), CT 06807. *Tel:* 203/629-2990. *Proprs:* David and Shulimin Block. *Hours:* Open all year, by appointment only.

A spacious office is home to 5000 volumes of highly specialized stock: press books, illustrated books, literature, and examples of fine printing and binding.

It is usual for shops carrying only rare and unusual specialties and little or no general stock to conduct business by appointment only. The very nature of uncommon specialties requires a quiet, unhurried atmosphere for examination and discussion.

Take Exit 4, Indian Field Rd. off I-95, turn right at Post Rd., then after one-fourth mile take a right turn at Strickland Rd., then 100 yards later turn right at Loughlin Ave.

Coventry

COVENTRY BOOK SHOP. 1159 Main St., Coventry, CT 06238. *Tel:* 203/742-9875. *Prop:* John Gambino. *Hours:* Open all year, Tuesday thru Sunday from 12:00 to 5:00.

Formerly the Book Corner in Manchester, this shop has about 10,000 general stock titles.

In Coventry, one-half mile south of junctions of Rtes. 31 and 275.

GIL SALK BOOKS AND BIRDS. 107B Jan Dr., Hebron, CT 06248 (mailing address), Mason St., Coventry, CT. *Tel:* 203/643-0380 (evenings only). *Hours:* Open all year, Saturday 1:00 to 4:00 and by appointment.

General stock of 10,000 volumes in all subjects. A growing specialty in bird books with a small stock of decoys and bird illustrations.

Mason St. is off Main St. (Rte. 31) opposite Coventry Library. Shop is in old mill and is unheated in winter.

East Hartford

THE BOOKIE. 116 Burnside Ave., East Hartford, CT 06108. *Tel:* 203/289-1208. *Prop:* Harold E. Kinney. *Hours:* Open all year Wednesday thru Sunday afternoons.

Most of the Bookie's stock consists of three specialties: science fiction, comic books for collectors and the increasingly popular early paperbacks. The stock is extensive numbering in the thousands and is well organized. The Bookie may well have the largest selection of science fiction and comic books for collectors in the area.

Burnside Ave. is the main artery in East Hartford.

Fairfield

JOHN SKUTEL GALLERIES/ANTIQUES-BOOKS. 45 Unquowa Rd., Fairfield, CT 06430. *Tel:* 203/255-9098. *Prop:* John Skutel. *Hours:* Open all year, Monday thru Saturday, 1:00 to 4:00 and by appointment.

This shop's general stock is supplied from approximately 50,000 volumes stored elsewhere. The stock includes much Americana.

In center of Fairfield off I-95.

THE MUSEUM GALLERY BOOK SHOP. Fairfield, CT 06490. *Tel:* 203/259-7114. *Prop:* Henry B. Caldwell. *Hours:* By appointment Tuesday thru Saturday from 2:00 to 5:00.

In 1982, Mr. Caldwell planned to move his stock of 10,000 books on fine arts, architecture, decorative arts, crafts and photography from a shop in Southport to his home in Fairfield. The phone number will be as shown above.

The shop's business has been conducted primarily with other well established dealers. When asked to consider welcoming the serious beginner, Mr. Caldwell replied, "I would like to encourage new book collectors... I have been depending on well established dealers, which can only make me think — that if they come to me, why shouldn't the beginner as well?"

Directions given with appointment.

Goshen

ANGLERS' AND SHOOTERS' BOOKSHELF. Goshen, CT 06756. *Prop:* Col. Henry A. Siegel. Mail order only.

Although this firm does not have the facilities for walk-in traffic, it does have possibly the largest collection of sporting books in North America.

Colonel Siegel issues what amounts to a handbook for the collector and other dealers in this traditional specialty, in catalogues that list 5000 select titles.

Catalogues are $5.00 a set on a one-time basis. Future catalogues will be sent if subscribers have ordered a reasonable number of titles.

The Bookshelf catalogues are indispensable for the novice and the long-time collector of sporting books.

Colonel Henry A. Siegel is co-author with Harry C. Marschalk, Jr., and Isaac Oelgart of what may be the definitive bibliography of the Derrydale Press from the Anglers' and Shooters' Press, Goshen, CT, 1981.

Middle Haddam

BIBLIOLATREE. Post Office Building, Rte. 151, Middle Haddam, CT 06456. *Tel:* 203/267-8222. *Hours:* Weekends, afternoons; weekdays, by chance.

This shop has stock of 10,000 volumes in American literature, history, children's books, bibliographical, nature and marine works, Western Americana, and some art.

A Huntsman

New Haven

WILLIAM REESE COMPANY. 409 Temple St., New Haven, CT 06511. *Tel:* 203/789-8081. *Prop:* William Reese. *Hours:* Open all year except August, an appointment is absolutely necessary.

The stock is highly specialized and for the most part rare and expensive. Specialties include western Americana and travel, colonial Americana and early imprints, 19th and 20th century American and British literature. The company has an unusually fine selection of titles on the Spanish Southwest and Mexico.

Bibliography, photographica, manuscript materials are all well represented.

Take Exit 3 off I-91, go straight on Trumball St. to second and third light close together, turn left at Temple and go half a block on left.

BRYN MAWR BOOK SHOP. 56½ Whitney Ave., New Haven, CT 06510. *Tel:* 203/562-4217. *Prop:* The Bryn Mawr Club of New Haven. *Hours:* Winter — Tuesday thru Friday 12 to 3:00, Saturday 10 to 1:00; Summer — Wednesday and Thursday 12 to 3:00; Closed last two weeks of August.

The Bryn Mawr Clubs in several cities have given up the traditional annual used book sale in favor of a year round scholarship fund raiser, the Bryn Mawr Book Shops.

Books are donated as is the work of the staff. Large donations receive charitable tax deductions. Collections from estates are often added to their stock.

Books are organized into categories in all subjects; excellent titles in art, science, history, biography and fiction.

Take Trumball St. exit from I-91, one-half block south of Trumball on Whitney.

WHITLOCK'S INCORPORATED. 15 Broadway, New Haven, CT 06511. *Tel:* 203/562-9841. *Prop:* Reverdy Whitlock. *Hours:* Monday thru Saturday 9:30 to 6:00.

Whitlock's was established in 1900 and through this century has supplied books to generations of the Yale and surrounding community.

Whitlock's has developed an extensive collection of Connecticut material and fine Americana.

One block from Yale's Sterling Memorial Library, easily reached from the expressway.

Newtown

THE PAGES OF YESTERYEAR. Old Hawleyville Rd., Newtown, CT 06470. *Tel:* 203/426-0864. *Prop:* John Renjilian. *Hours:* By appointment.

Stock covers juveniles including "Street Literature," i.e., chapbooks, toy books, broadsides, song sheets. Some excellent "courtesy" books and "upward bound" titles are included. These guides to worldly success were popular in 19th Century America where an agricultural society was swiftly changing to a commercial and industrial one.

Books on household management and the domestic arts, sports and games, pre-20th Century, and other materials illustrating daily life are included in stock. This shop has fine collections of rare books on history and exploration, travel, science and medicine, and Americana. Also included are miniature books, and books on art, photography and illustrations.

The stock of 25,000 items is in the barn for browsing by appointment, but as in shops with regular hours, valuable items are separate from the general stock.

Directions given with appointment.

Stratford

FINE LITERARY PROPERTY. 752A Pontiac La., Oronoque Village, Stratford, CT 06497. *Tel:* 203/375-9073. *Prop:* Preston C. Beyer. *Hours:* By mail order and appointment.

Beyer's specialties are modern literary firsts, books about books, fine press books, poetry, American expatriate authors printed in the U.S. and Europe 1920-39 and "little magazines."

Beyer's catalogues ($2.00) are, like many dealer catalogues, a bargain at twenty times the price. Catalogue No. 21 has 175 items listed for John Steinbeck including bibliographies and foreign editions.

Directions given by mail or phone.

Torrington

NUTMEG BOOKS. 5 Water St., Box 85, Torrington, CT 06790. *Tel:* 203/482-8870 or 482-9696. *Proprs:* Bill and Debby Goring. *Hours:* Open all year, Tuesday thru Saturday from 12 to 5:00.

This second floor shop has seven rooms full of books. Walk-in customers, dealers and specialty collectors find titles of interest in Nutmeg's general stock of used, out of print and rare books.

Browsers are welcome and the coffee pot is usually on.

Roughly in the center of town. Water St. joins Main St., as well as South Main and East Main Sts. In fact, Water St. might be considered West Main St.

West Cornwall

BARBARA FARNSWORTH — BOOKS. Rte. 128, West Cornwall, CT 06796. *Tel:* 203/672-6333 — shop, 203/672-6571 — home. *Hours:* By chance or appointment.

This book shop is in a large two story barn, but there is nothing barn-like in the attractive interior. A clean, light place, books are arranged alphabetically within categories on shelves that are separated by wide aisles.

A general stock of about 50,000 books is on the shelves here with a large selection of fine illustrated books and excellent 19th Century American and English books, fiction, biography, history.

One hundred yards east on Rte. 128 from the covered bridge on Rte. 7.

DEBORAH BENSON — BOOKSELLER. River Rd., West Cornwall, CT 06796. *Tel:* 203/672-6614. *Hours:* Open all year, call ahead for directions.

Stock numbers about 13,000 volumes, including a distinguished collection of detective fiction in first editions.

There are books about books. When collecting these, you will learn that "enough is too much" does not apply. There is always room for one or one hundred more books about books on your shelves. I have never met a conscientious dealer or collector, however knowledgeable, who did not at some time express dis-

Type Founding. Inking Balls. Work at Press. Correcting Errors. Proof Reading. Composing.

satisfaction with his own knowledge of books.

Medical texts and literature are enjoying a surge in popularity and Benson's is well represented with a strong collection in early opthalmology. Fore-edge painting is causing a flurry beyond the circle of long-time dedicated fore-edge painting collectors, and Benson has some of the finest examples of this book decorating art. There are children's books, both contemporary and old fashioned, paper ephemera in many subjects, and a small, thoughtfully chosen general stock, including first editions.

Maine

Alfred

ROBERT CANNEY — RARE BOOKS. PO Box 350, Alfred Sq., Alfred, ME 04022. *Tel:* 207/324-6292. *Prop:* Robert Canney. *Hours:* April thru October only, by appointment.

Stock is very well chosen and includes local histories, atlases, maps, first editions, color plates, view books.

On Rtes. 202 and 4 opposite the village green in Alfred.

Anson

COLBY SEAMS — BOOKS. PO Box 66, Anson, ME 04911. *Prop:* Colby Seams. *Hours:* By chance or appointment, open all year.

Shop has 8000 volumes of literature, history, mystery and Maine titles.

Just off Rte. 201-A in Anson. Take Hwy. 139 West off Maine Turnpike.

Bangor

PRO LIBRIS. 33 Franklin St., Bangor, ME 04401. *Tel:* 207/942-3019. *Prop:* Eric Furry. *Hours:* Open all year, Monday thru Saturday 10 to 5:30.

With ten years experience in bookselling, Mr. Furry established Pro Libris in 1980. The stock, mass market and trade paperbacks, numbers 20,000; shop specialties are literature, science fiction, westerns, and avant-garde literature.

Next to the rear of Sunbury Mall in downtown Bangor.

Bethel

BETHEL BOOK BARN. Lower Main St., Box 353, Bethel, ME 04217. *Tel:* 207/824-3145. *Prop:* Dan Cousens. *Hours:* Open 7 days and evenings thru Fall Foliage.

General stock of 15,000 volumes, with emphasis on history and biography and a growing collection of literature. The Barn also carries several thousand titles in philosophy, religion, psychology, economics and sociology.

"Attention is given to orderly shelving to insure easy browsing in a relaxed atmosphere."

Bethel is on the edge of the White Mountain National Forest at the intersection of Rtes. 5 and 35 and Hwy. 2. The Book Barn is on lower Main St. next to Martha's Restaurant.

Bingham

BILL LIPPINCOTT BOOKS. Box 506, Main St., Bingham, ME 04920. *Tel:* 207/672-4888, 207/566-7972 (Home). *Prop:* Bill Lippincott. *Hours:* All year, Tuesday thru Saturday 9:30 to 5:00.

Another favorite. Lippincott has a well chosen general stock including sound titles in hunting, fishing, Maine books, mystery and science fiction.

Good selection of children's books here: Oz, Uncle Remus, and early Seuss books like the great *500 Hats of Bartholomew Cubbins.* The shop carries serial books like Tom Swift, Tarzan and Nancy Drew.

Lippincott started out with comic books and still carries a selection of better comics, pulps and vintage paperbacks.

Take I-95 (Maine Turnpike) north to Rte. 201 (about 20 miles north of Augusta). Take Rte. 201A northwest through some of the loveliest, unspoiled country in Maine.

Brewer

MEDICAL BOOK SERVICE COMPANY. Box 447, Brewer, ME 04401. *Tel:* 207/843-5052. *Prop:* Jon B. Johansen. *Hours:* By appointment.

Specializing in antique and out of print medical books and periodicals, this firm also does book binding.

Brewer is right outside Bangor. Specific directions given with appointment.

Bridgton

BRIDGTON BOOK HOUSE. Depot St., Bridgton, ME 04009. *Prop:* Sawyer E. Medbury. *Hours:* Last week of June thru Saturday of Labor Day weekend; weekdays 10 to 4:30, Saturday 10 to 1:00; closed Wednesday and Sunday.

The Book House has a general stock of 5000 books, mostly classics, in hard cover and paperback.

Just off Rte. 302 on Depot St. next to the Magic Lantern Theatre. The Shop's sign is on 302.

Brunswick

WALFIELD-THISTLE, INC. 381 Bath Rd., Brunswick, ME 04011. *Tel:* 207/443-3986. *Hours:* Open all year daily from 10 to 5:00; closed Sunday, other times by appointment.

There are over 4000 volumes in this shop, in all categories.

Two miles east from Cook's Corner off Rte. 1 on Bath Rd., East Brunswick.

Bryant Pond

MOLL OCKETT ANTIQUES. Rte. 26, Box 36, Bryant Pond, ME 04219. *Tel:* Bryant Pond 80. *Prop:* Starr Seguin. *Hours:* June thru August, Thursday thru Sunday 11 to 5:00; April and May, September and October, weekends.

Most subjects are represented in over 5000 books in this shop, with specialties in Maine and New England titles. Much paper ephemera — postcards, advertising material, catalogues, etc.

Take Rte. 26 from Gray exit. Bryant Pond is between Woodstock and Bethel. Rte. 26 is a rural Book Row, with Anna's in South Paris, Moll Ockett's and the Book Barn in Bethel.

Buckfield

PATRICIA LEDLIE — BOOKSELLER. Box 46, Buckfield, ME 04220. *Prop:* Patricia Ledlie. *Hours:* Mail Order.

Ledlie's specialty is natural history. Catalogues are issued three times a year with fine titles on birds, fish, reptiles and mammals. Send a stamped, self-addressed postal card for catalogue prices.

Cundy's Harbor

BOOK PEDLARS. Holbrook St., Cundy's Harbor, ME 04011. *Tel:* 207/729-0087. *Proprs:* Wally and Laura O'Brien. *Hours:* June thru August from 11 to 5:00 daily, Spring and Fall on weekends from 11 to 5:00, otherwise by appointment.

The proprietors suggest calling before visiting, but since they live next door, will open up at any reasonable time. They have 4000 volumes of general stock including Americana, fiction, art, fishing, New England and biography. They specialize in Maine titles and Children's illustrated books.

Eight miles from Cook's Corner, Brunswick. Go 4 miles south on Rte. 24 to Cundy's Harbor Rd. on left, then 4 miles to Holbrook St. "Book Pedlars" sign on corner.

Eustis

MACDONALD'S MILITARY MEMORABILIA AND MAINE MEMENTOES. Rte. 27, Eustis, ME 04936. *Tel:* 207/297-2751. *Prop:* Tom MacDonald. *Hours:* By appointment.

MacDonald's specialty is Civil War titles. The shop has 5000 volumes.

In the North Country past Sugarloaf. Specific directions given with appointment.

Freeport

BOOK CELLAR. 36 Main St. (Rte. 1), Freeport, ME 04032. *Tel:* 207/865-3157. *Prop:* Dean Chamberlin. *Hours:* Visitors always welcome, call ahead if coming from a distance.

The Book Cellar stocks 25,000 books with specialties in children's, nostalgic fiction, biography, and a growing specialty in books about dolls. The shop's business is conducted mostly by mail, but customers are always welcomed if they call ahead.

Mr. Chamberlain publishes a list of Maine dealers for "visiting out-of-state dealers, visitors, and anyone else interested in old books." There is no charge for this list but you must send a stamped envelope.

Gardiner

BUNKHOUSE BOOKS. Rte. 5A—Gardiner-Lewiston Rd., Gardiner, ME 04345. *Tel:* 207/582-2808. *Prop:* Isaac Davis, Jr. *Hours:* May thru October from 12 to 9:00, otherwise by appointment.

The Bunkhouse has one of the largest collections of Maine town histories, as well as Maine non-fiction titles and books by Maine authors. The shop has 15,000 volumes that include sporting and military books and general Americana.

Mr. Davis keeps a file of books in stock right by the telephone, so phone orders are handled quickly.

Take Gardiner exit from Maine turnpike, three-fourths of mile west on Rte. 126.

Kennebunk

THE OLD BOOK SHOP. 61 York St. (U.S. 1), Kennebunk, ME 04043. *Tel:* 207/985-3748. *Proprs:* Tom and Viola Drysdale. *Hours:* Spring thru Fall open daily from 9 to 9:00, call at house in winter.

About 50,000 volumes, general stock, including Maine and New England titles and the works of Kenneth Roberts.

You have to look sharp on this stretch with its mix of antique and craft stalls, motels, restaurants, and private residences.

On the left going north on U.S. 1.

Lewiston

DEBORAH ISAACSON, BOOKSELLER. 11 Ash St., Box 932, Lewiston, ME 04240. *Tel:* 207/784-3937. *Prop:* Deborah Isaacson. *Hours:* Daily 11 to 5:00, closed Wednesday and Sunday.

This shop carries a general stock with emphasis on the arts. There is a large selection of science fiction and fantasy. There is also an inventory of prints.

In downtown Lewiston between Lisbon and Canal Sts., next to a car park.

Litchfield

MAURICE OWEN — BOOKS. Bowdoin Center Rd., RFD 2, Litchfield, ME 04350. *Tel:* 207/268-4206. *Prop:* Maurice Owen. *Hours:* By appointment.

The general stock in this shop includes westerns, mysteries, adventure and romance. Specialty is in the increasingly popular boys and girls series such as

Campfire Girls, Trixie Belden, The Boy Allies and Tom Swift.

Directions given with appointment.

Manchester

CHARLES ROBINSON RARE BOOKS. Pond Rd., Box 57, Manchester, ME 04351. *Tel:* 207/622-1885. *Prop:* Charles Robinson. *Hours:* By appointment, Readers Annex open June 1 thru October 15.

The shop's specialties are illustrated books, fine bindings, Western Americana, science, medicine, modern first editions, travel and exploration.

Mr. Robinson, Vice-President of the Maine Antiquarian Booksellers Association, conducts annual rare book auctions.

Manchester is 5 miles from the Maine Turnpike, exit 15N at Augusta. Specific directions given with appointment.

North Berwick

DOUGHTY'S FALLS OLD BOOKSHOP. Rte. 9, North Berwick, ME 03906. *Tel:* 207/976-4490. *Proprs:* Bill and Eleanor Riviere. *Hours:* April-November daily from 10 to 9:00.

Over 7000 volumes with specialties in hunting, fishing and Maine titles.

Take Wells exit from Maine Turnpike onto Rte. 9, turn left (east) towards Rte. 1. Shop is on left outside town of Wells. Proprietors take a day off occasionally, so a call ahead is advisable.

North Edgecomb

EDGECOMB BOOK BARN. Cross Point Rd., North Edgecomb, ME 04556. *Tel:* 207/882-7278. *Proprs:* Frank, Maggie, Kim and Kevin McQuaid. *Hours:* Summer, daily 11 to 6:00; winter, by appointment.

There are over 30,000 volumes in this bookbarn, with specialties in the illustrated book, children's, marine, Americana and Maine titles.

Turn off Rte. 1 onto Rte. 27 to Boothbay Harbor. Turn right one mile from Rte. 1.

Pittsfield

WINTER FARM BOOKS. RFD 2, Box 540, Pittsfield, ME 04967. *Tel:* 207/938-4141. *Prop:* Robert K. Foote. *Hours:* By mail order and appointment.

So far Winter Farms has issued three catalogues on their specialty, non-fiction Maine titles including town and county histories, genealogies, atlases, vital records, and personal narratives. They contain one of the largest selections of sought-after Maine books; the bibliographic descriptions are unusually thorough.

Winter Farms catalogues are invaluable for the reader/collector in this specialty. They are also well printed and a pleasure to read. Catalogues are one dollar each.

Directions given with appointment.

Portland

F. M. O'BRIEN — ANTIQUARIAN BOOKSELLER. 34 and 36 High St., Portland, ME 04101. *Tel:* 207/774-0931. *Prop:* F. M. O'Brien. *Hours:* Open all year Monday thru Saturday, 10:30 to 5:30, and by appointment.

A venerable. O'Brien's was established in 1934 and has one of the largest stocks in Maine. In addition to general titles, American, English and foreign literature, the shop carries autographs, historical documents, pamphlets, American prints and paintings. Maine books are a specialty.

High St. is a principal cross-town street beginning at the waterfront. The shop is five houses up from the foot on the left.

Round Pond

CARRIAGE HOUSE. Rte. 32, Round Pond, ME 04564. *Tel:* 207/529-5555. *Prop:* Roy Gillespie. *Hours:* Summer 8 to 5:00 daily, winter by chance or appointment.

The Carriage House has a general stock of about 3000 volumes.

The shop is on Rte. 32 one mile south of Round Pond.

Sanford

THE BOOK ADDICT. Box 1281, Pinetree Dr., Sanford, ME 04073. *Tel:* 207/324-2243. *Prop:* David A. Foshey. *Hours:* Mail order and by appointment from May thru October.

There are 2500 volumes in the Book Addict, some general stock, with emphasis on sports, biography and history.

Directions with appointment.

Skowhegan

BOOK LOFT. 178 Madison Ave., Skowhegan, ME 04976. *Tel:* 207/474-3185. *Prop:* Robert Chandler. *Hours:* Wednesday thru Friday 1 to 5:00, but call ahead.

Specialties at the Book Loft are juvenile series (Boy's) and Maine titles.

The shop is near McDonald's and Whittemore's Restaurant.

South Casco

VARNEY'S VOLUMES. Quaker Ridge Rd., Casco, ME 04015. *Tel:* 207/655-4605 or 655-4917. *Prop:* Lois Varney. *Hours:* July and August, daily 10 to 5:00, closed Wednesday and Sunday; mail order and by appointment all year.

Varney's has a general stock of about 7000 volumes with emphasis on juveniles, Maine titles, history, nostalgic fiction.

Casco is Varney's mailing address. The shop is located in South Casco just off Rte. 302 opposite Thomas Inn, close by Sebago Lake.

South China

M. CHARLES BOOKS. South China, ME 04358. *Tel:* 207/445-2245. *Prop:* M. Charles. *Hours:* Open all year, advisable to call ahead, 10 to 5:00 daily.

A general stock of about 9800 well chosen titles.

South China is 10 miles east of Augusta on Rte. 202 — 9 — 3. Specific directions with appointment.

South Paris

ANNA'S BOOKS. 17 Church St., South Paris, ME 04281. *Proprs:* Charles and Anna Johnson. *Hours:* Open all year when proprietors are home "which we usually are."

Part of the stock is located in the stable, with the balance in the Johnson home. Stock is general including New England authors and town and country histories.

Exit from Maine Turnpike at Gray. Take Rte. 26 to Norway-Paris. Church St. intersects Main St. There is a granite Methodist Church on corner, brick town library on opposite corner. Book shop sign is on stable.

Springvale

THE BOOKBARN. 286 Main St. (Rte. 109), Springvale, ME 04083. *Tel:* 207/324-8255. *Prop:* Allen Scott. *Hours:* June 1 thru Labor Day, 10 to 10:00 (but best to call after 5:00), September thru May by appointment.

I must admit to a strong prejudice for the Bookbarn. The stock moves, so there is always a new cache to plunder. Mr. Scott teaches English at a nearby college and his literature titles have a breadth and quality that will gratify the most discriminating reader-collector. Fine first editions, but even the reading copies here are mint with clean dust jackets.

Books are catalogued by subject in alphabetical order. This is a clean, well lighted, shipshape bookbarn. There are over 25,000 volumes divided into sought after specialties: nature, history, art, medicine, pyschology, religion, the occult and Americana. There are good music history titles and hard to find books on books and book auction catalogues.

Take the Wells exit off the Maine Turnpike, go west on 109, through Sanford, through Springvale center. Barn is attached to house on left.

FRANK WOOD — BOOKS. 256 Main St., Box 365, Springvale, ME 04083. *Tel:* 207/324-8319. *Prop:* Frank Wood. *Hours:* By mail and appointment.

The shop's specialties are Maine, Americana and communal material. New England has always been a rich source of communal subjects, with its Shakers and Fruitlands, right up to the present where communal societies born in the 1960s are still flourishing or languishing according to the commitment of members. Louisa May Alcott wrote amusingly of the Fruitlands experiment in *Transcendental Wild Oats,* but her journal and the letters and diary of her mother reveal a darker side of the Fruitlands experiment. The shop has Shaker material and less well known Utopian titles.

Mr. Wood is another example of the diverse backgrounds of New England booksellers. He has served his district in the Maine House and is presently in the Maine Senate.

Shop is one block west of Nasson College.

HARLAND EASTMAN, BOOKS. 66 Main St., Springvale, ME 04083. *Tel:* 207/324-2797. *Hours:* No set hours, proprietor usually home. Appointment not necessary.

Shop is in remodeled barn loft, inviting, well-lighted. Mr. Eastman specializes in Victorian and Edwardian children's books and his selections are superb. Eastman carries a well chosen general stock and a wide selection of Maine titles, fiction and non-fiction, and a nearly complete collection of Maine town histories. Because of the scarcity of some of these early histories, Eastman has begun re-issuing a few of the more sought after town histories.

With three fine used bookshops, Main St. is becoming Springvale's Brick Row.

Spruce Head

LOBSTER LANE BOOK SHOP. Spruce Head, ME 04859. *Tel:* 207/594-7520. *Prop:* Vivian York. *Hours:* June 12 thru September 30 from 12:30 to 5:00, seven days.

This is an orderly shop of about 25,000 volumes. Fiction is catalogued by author alphabetically, non-fiction by subject. Lobster Lane is a regular stop for summer visitors, collectors and those looking for fine nature books or old out-of-print children's books.

Ms. York suggests that if you are coming from a long distance it is advisable to call ahead.

One of the special delights of book hunting in Maine is the chance to see coastal and inland villages the developers (destroyers) have overlooked.

Right after passing thru Thomaston's Main St. (U.S. 1) going north, you will see the General Knox mansion on a rise on right. Turn there onto Rte. 131, keep going until Rte. 73, where you turn left.

Steep Falls

NELLIE WARD'S BOOKBARN. Rtes. 11 and 113, Box 6, Steep Falls, ME 04085. *Tel:* 207/675-3348. *Hours:* Tuesday thru Thursday and Saturday 8 to 5:00 and by appointment.

This bookbarn specializes in out-of-print books in many different subjects.

Take exit 8 off the Maine Turnpike onto Rte. 25 to Rte. 13. The bookbarn is near the intersection of Rtes. 11 and 113.

Wells

DOUGLAS N. HARDING — RARE BOOKS. Box 184, Rte. 1, Webhannet Farm, Wells, ME 04090. *Tel:* 207/646-8785. *Hours:* Advisable to call ahead.

Specialties in natural history, travel, view books, Arctic and Canada. Harding has some fine botany and ornithology titles beautifully illustrated. Small general stock.

Shop is in remodeled, attached barn one mile north of Wells Corner on the ocean side of Rte. 1.

West Jonesport

JONESPORT WOOD CO., INC./MOOSABEC REACH HISTORICAL CO., Main St., PO Box 295, West Jonesport, ME 04649. *Tel:* 207/497-2322. *Prop:* Skip Brack. *Hours:* Daily 9 to 5:00, June 15 thru September 15; Thursday thru Saturday 9 to 5:00, Sunday p.m. rest of year.

I'm not certain, but this shop may be the only shop in New England accessible by boat. The Wood Company carries prints and books in addition to old woodworking tools. The Historical Company in the next building has a gallery, print shops and more books.

The shop's illustrated catalogue is an excellent one for beginners. Book and print descriptions are thorough, and there is an explanatory list of the abbreviations used. It is worth more than the three dollar price.

General stock in all shops with specialties in Americana, New England and Maine titles, nature, exploration, marine, early architecture, fiction, history, etc.

You will daydream about this shop all winter; it is that memorable.

West Jonesport is way down, past Bar Harbor. Stay on Rte. 1 until Rte. 187 near Addison, turn right.

Winthrop

MIRKWOOD BOOKS. RFD 3 North Wayne, Winthrop, ME 04364. *Tel:* 207/685-3860. *Prop:* Joan Chellis. *Hours:* From end of mud season until heavy snowfall, daily from 11 to 5:00 and some evenings.

"Mirkwood Books is a reader's bookshop," with about 6000 books. Subjects include Maine, mysteries, children's, biographies and nature. The shop is hard to find, but worth the jaunt. The proprietor offers free tea and good books in a lovely setting.

Seven miles from Winthrop. Take Rte. 133 for four miles, turn right onto North Wayne Rd., go right at end of road. Shop is ¾ mile up the hill. Follow signs to Tall Timbers.

Massachusetts

Adams

SECOND LIFE BOOKS. Upper East Hoosac St., Adams, MA 01220. *Tel:* 413/743-4561. *Proprs:* Russell and Martha Freedman. *Hours:* Summer Tuesday thru Sunday 10 to 5:00 and by appointment; winter by appointment only.

An impressive general stock numbering 20 to 25,000 and equally impressive collections of specialties that are increasingly popular with younger collectors especially women — feminism, American reform movements are only a few of the shop's subject specialties. Traditionally, women have been an almost invisible presence in the rare/used book trade as collectors and booksellers. This is changing rapidly.

Women booksellers are bringing to the trade the meticulous scholarship of university training, and the financial acumen of the business world. The current president of the Antiquarian Booksellers Association of America is Elisabeth Woodburn, proprietor of Booknoll Farm, Hopewell, New Jersey.

Go north on Rte. 8, take first right after statue of William McKinley. The shop is 1½ miles up the hill, on the right.

Amherst

VALLEY BOOKSHOP. 5 East Pleasant St., Amherst, MA 01002. *Tel:* 413/549-6052. *Prop:* Larry Pruner. *Hours:* Open all year, Monday thru Saturday 10 to 5:30, Sunday 12 to 5:00.

Another excellent shop for the collector, the home library builder, and area college students and faculty. A stock of over 30,000 books, most of which are classics and sought after titles in all fields at moderate prices. In this shop you will find first and limited editions in the low to medium price range, the literature of other cultures, and most importantly, of our own. I say this not from chauvinism, but in recognition of the scarcity of standard titles by our own authors, Hawthorne, Irving, Twain, Parkman, in affordable, readable editions.

It is disturbing that a country's cultural past is distorted, if not obliterated by the unavailability to the public of the literary works that shaped that culture. We owe much to our used book sellers for saving these neglected works.

From the south, take Amherst exit off Rte. 1-95, Rte. 9 west to the town center. From the north, Sutherland exit off Rte. 91, the 11 B south. East or west, Mass. pike to 91 exit north, Rte. 91 to Amherst exit, Rte. 9 to center of town.

Bedford

DUNHAM'S BOOKSTORE. 50 Great Rd., Rtes. 4 — 225 — 62, Bedford, MA 01730. *Tel:* 617/275-9140. *Proprs:* Carroll and Grace Dunham. *Hours:* Open all year except last two weeks of August, Tuesday thru Saturday 10:30 to 5:30 and Friday evening 7 to 9:00.

In business over twenty years, Dunham's has a general stock of 20,000 books in good to very fine condition. Titles cover all subjects, fiction and non-fiction, from standard titles and scarce out-of-print, to rare books.

Dunham's carries an interesting and varied selection of sheet music, comics, post cards. There are some historically valuable sepia tint photo-cards of towns and cities as well as the sought after "holiday" or "high tack" postcards with their garish colors and risque verses. There is also a nice selection of stereopticon cards.

All stock in this orderly shop is categorized.

Belmont

PAYSON HALL BOOKSHOP. 80 Trapelo Rd., Belmont, MA 02178. *Tel:* 617/484-2020. *Prop:* Clare M. Murphy. *Hours:* Open all year, Tuesday thru Saturday 10 to 5:00.

The shop is in an Old-English style building, with leaded glass bow windows. A pleasant, well-lighted place with a general stock of approximately 10,000 hardcover books. Some unusually interesting early to late 19th century titles.

Beverly

JEAN S. MCKENNA — BOOKS. PO Box 397, 131 Dodge St., Rte. 1A, Beverly, MA 01915. *Tel:* 617/927-3067. *Prop:* Jean S. McKenna. *Hours:* Open all year, Tuesday thru Saturday 12 to 5:00.

A varied general stock including area and local histories with specialties in children's and illustrated books. McKenna's children's section shows real discernment in its selection of titles old and new. Avoid this shop if you can't stay around a while. Not only does McKenna welcome browsers, her stock captivates them. There are duplicates here so you may purchase, say, a collectible first edition of George MacDonald's "The Light Princess" and the 1962 Crowell edition as a reading copy. Come to think of it, the Crowell edition is illustrated by William Pene DuBois, and in good condition is collectible itself. In any case, there are reading or "working" copies here, as well as suitable collection copies.

Take exit 20 north off Rte. 128. The shop is about ½ mile down Rte. 1-A on the right.

Boston

BOSTON BOOK ANNEX. 906 Beacon St., Boston, MA 02215. *Tel:* 617/266-1090. *Proprs:* Francine L. Ness and Helen Kelly. *Hours:* Open all year, all week from 10 to 8:00, Sunday from 10 to 5:00.

An unusually wide range of excellent first editions in sought-after titles. Book Annex carries those sets that booksellers could not give away ten years ago, but are now sought after, not only by specialty collectors but for the home library. The complete works of Dickens, George Eliot, Jane Austen, Hawthorne, Melville, Twain and so on are included.

Bless Book Annex for staying open on Sunday.

BRATTLE BOOK SHOP. 25 West St., Boston, MA 02215. *Tel:* 617/542-0210. *Proprs:* George and Kenneth Gloss. *Hours:* Open all year, Monday thru Saturday.

Probably the most well known bookshop in Boston, not only to the bibliophile but to the general public, the Brattle has defied fire, politically expedient if ineffectual redistricting, and the wrecking ball of urban renewal to retain its title "Successor to America's Oldest Continuous Antiquarian Bookshop."

In 1945 George Gloss purchased the Brattle, founded in 1825, at its original site in the Cornhill district, present site of Boston's Government Center.

The Brattle is one of the least intimidating shops for the beginning collector. Scholars, students, musicians, actors, writers, salesclerks, artists, bankers, bartenders, anyone who loves books, is at home at the Brattle.

The general stock is as varied and interesting as the patrons. Specialties in Americana, the illustrated book, Boston, New England, juveniles, natural history, nautical books, first editions, American and European fiction, and sets, are well represented.

For many bibliophiles, it is not Boston, but the Brattle, that is the hub of their universe.

BROMER BOOKSELLERS. 607 Boylston St. (at Copley Sq.), Boston, MA 02116. *Tel:* 617/247-2818. *Proprs:* Anne and David Bromer. *Hours:* Monday thru Friday, 9:30 to 5:30; other times by appointment.

That beautifully made books are cherished here is apparent in the way the Bromers display their examples of the Book Arts — fine printing, illustrations, binding. "We view the book as an artifact and are extremely fussy about condition, presenting only the best-preserved copies of books and related items."

The Bromers' collection of books and related items numbers about 5000, with specialties in rare, private press and illustrated books, fine first editions, juveniles and miniature books, usually 3 inches and under. They are major dealers in miniature books, and are considered by dealers and collectors alike to be experts in this field.

EDWARD MORRILL AND SONS, INC. 25 Kingston St., Boston, MA 02111. *Tel:* 617/482-3090. *Hours:* All year, Monday thru Friday 8:30 to 3:30.

Another venerable. Morrill's carries fine out of print and rare books with specialties in Americana, foreign travel and the arts.

GOODSPEED'S BOOK SHOP. 7 Beacon St. and 2 Milk St., Boston, MA 02108. *Tel:* 617/523-5970. *Prop:* George Goodspeed. *Hours:* Monday thru Friday 9 to 5:00; September to June open Saturday 10 to 3:00; closed Saturdays in Summer.

In *A Writer's Capital,* Louis Auchincloss writes, "In Boston I began what has been a minor subchapter, or perhaps footnote, to my literary career. I made my first purchase as a collector of rare books. At Goodspeed's, I spied a set of Jane Austen, mostly in first edition. I decided all of a sudden that I wanted these more than anything in the world and that I wanted them on board my ship."

What happened to the set of Ms. Austen's works makes poignant reading. But also of interest is that Mr. Auchincloss writes "at Goodspeed's." To add "Book Shop" is unnecessary.

DEVICE OF CHRISTOPHER PLANTIN, "KING OF PRINTERS."
From a book of 1588.

155

Since 1898 when Charles E. Goodspeed opened his bookshop on Park St., Goodspeed's has been known for the quality and integrity of its collections and the scholarship of its staff.

The stock at 2 Milk St. includes titles in art, architecture, ships and the sea, natural history, biography and the social sciences.

Goodspeed's at 7 Beacon St. houses their collections of rare Americana, English and American literature, early printing, autograph letters and manuscripts, genealogy and local history, old lithographs and engravings.

General stocks also at both shops.

STARR BOOK COMPANY, INC. 186 South St., Boston, MA 02111. *Tel:* 617/542-2525. *Proprs:* Norman B. Starr, Ernest D. Starr. *Hours:* Open all year, Monday thru Friday 9 to 5:00, Saturday 9 to 4:00.

Boston's Starr Book Company has 150,000 thoughtfully chosen books in all subject areas. Specialties include American and English fiction of every period. This Boston shop's fiction collection shows an unusual breadth and depth. You can see along the shelves the development of our own literary tradition; colonialism, the genteel tradition, the rough regionalism, the vigorous, sometimes strange attempts to wrest a vision from what Miss Cather called, "not a country, but the material from which countries are made."

Starr has an impressive collection of sets of standard works by American and English authors. You can find sets in most bookshops but here you can choose from different editions.

I have two sets of Dickens's collected works. The Booklover's Edition was published by the University Society, New York, in 1908, illustrated. A "Life and Critical Estimate" is included with introductions by Andrew Lang, Charles Dickens the younger, and others; there are also essays by Gissing, Chesterton, Swinburne.

The books in this set measure a compact 4½ by 7 inches and are less than an inch thick. These are handsome, sturdy little books with green leatherette covers, brave in gilt as Bob Cratchett's wife was brave in her Christmas ribbons. I consider this set a "working" set. It has been well used through three generations of Dickens worshippers and the books are still tightly bound and in good to fine condition.

The other set of Dickens has thicker volumes, of larger size, elaborately bound in leather. Their papers are so richly dense the print seems incised into their surfaces.

This is not a "working" set, but neither is it idle.

The books in this set are affordable examples of the book as an art object, and the pleasure their heft and loveliness affords is almost voluptuous. Reading from this set of the works of an author who has engaged my sympathy and affection throughout my life adds another dimension to my enjoyment of Dickens.

Get a good, tightly bound and complete set of an author's work in a serviceable edition, then seek out finer editions.

Cambridge

BRYN MAWR BOOK SALE. 373 Huron Ave., Cambridge, MA 02138. *Tel:* 617/661-1770. *Hours:* All year, Tuesday thru Saturday 10 to 5:00.

Another Bryn Mawr scholarship fundraiser, staffed by volunteers. There is a general stock of more than 10,000 volumes with some rare and hard to find out of print books. Shop occasionally receives fine collections as donations. There is a half price sale in the spring, and books are marked down regularly all year.

GROLIER BOOK SHOP. 6 Plympton St., Cambridge, MA 02138. *Tel:* 617/547-4648. *Prop:* Louisa Solano. *Hours:* All year, Tuesday thru Friday 10 to 6:00, Saturday 10 to 5:30.

A venerable, but with a difference. Grolier is the oldest continuing bookshop in America specializing in poetry. Shop stocks about 10,000 books by and about poets.

Solano is evangelical about poetry, co-sponsoring the annual Grolier Poetry Prize and starting the Grolier Reading Series as well as sponsoring the Grolier Rimes softball and basketball teams.

The Grolier carries the poetry of small presses. All used book shops should carry some small press titles. There is more vigorous and original writing being done in small presses than anywhere else.

Concord

THE BARROW BOOKSTORE. 79 Main St., Concord, MA 01742. *Tel:* 617/369-6084. *Prop:* Clairborne Dawes. *Hours:* Open all year, Monday thru Saturday 9:30 to 5:00.

This bright, spacious shop opened in 1971. It has a carefully chosen general stock of about 20,000 books. The shop, appropriately enough, specializes in the Concord authors — Thoreau, Emerson, Hawthorne, the Alcotts and others. The Barrow has an exceptionally good selection of children's books, including many different editions of *Little Women* and other Louisa May Alcott titles. Miss Alcott's *Life, Letters and Journal* edited by Ednah D. Cheney, Boston, Roberts Brothers, 1890, reveals the harsh imperatives of poverty under which Miss Alcott labored unremittingly well past middle age. She writes of her life as she lived it, with great courage and dignity. She never whined; she faced denial, cold and want, her own doubts about her abilities, and her fame, with grace and fortitude. The Letters and Journals should be required reading for young people as an example of how to be courageous and useful.

Barrow Book Shop is in the center of Concord. Look for their wooden wheelbarrow in front of the shop. In good weather the wheelbarrow overflows with paperback books.

Gardner

IRENE'S BOOK SHOP. 49 West Broadway, Gardner, MA 01440. *Tel:* 617/632-5574. *Prop:* Irene M. Walet. *Hours:* Open April to October, Monday thru Friday 1 to 5:00, Saturday and Sunday by appointment.

This shop has 30,000 volumes of used and op books in all categories. From October to April, the shop is closed but sale lists are sent out during the winter months. The proprietor plans to conduct book auctions in the future.

When requesting book lists from dealers who do not charge for catalogues or lists, send SASE.

Gloucester

TEN POUND ISLAND BOOK COMPANY. 93 Main St., Gloucester, MA 01930. *Tel:* 617/283-5299 or 283-7312 or 281-3864. *Proprs:* Jean Radoslovich and Gregory Gibson. *Hours:* Summer, Monday thru Saturday 10 to 5:00, Sunday 1 to 5:00; winter, Monday thru Saturday 12 to 5:00, Sunday 1 to 5:00; other times by appointment.

Named for an island in Gloucester Harbor the shop was established in 1976. A general stock of 15,000 books, old, scarce and out of print in all subject areas. This shop has a women's studies section including women writers of all periods — Aphra Ben, Margaret Fuller, de Beauvoir. No serious student of women's studies should neglect the 19th century and earlier books on the education and treatment of women. Examples: *What Can A Woman Do, or Her Position in the Business and Literary World* by Mrs. M.L. Rayne, 1884; the thoughtful, and for its time, 1851, radical book by William Hosmer with its deceptively mild title *The Young Lady's Book or Principles of Female Education.*

The shop carries fine arts titles, and local and area history is well represented. A sound collection of maritime titles is here. For maritime collectors, the shop issues lists in this specialty throughout the year. Remember to enclose SASE when sending for lists or any information.

Take Gloucester exit from Rte. 128; shop is in downtown Gloucester.

Harwich

STATEN HOOK BOOKS. 705 Main St., Harwich, MA 02645. *Tel:* 617/432-2155. *Hours:* June to September, Monday thru Saturday 11 to 5:00; October to May, Saturday 11 to 5:00.

Staten Hook Books has a large general stock with specialties in marine titles, fishing, and Cape Cod. Some interesting paper ephemera, good selection of periodicals.

Located in Harwich Center. An inviting shop front. Two, large, many-paned windows flank the entrance. The shop's sign is prominently displayed.

Huntington

THE COOKERY BOOKERY. Worthington Rd., Huntington, MA 01050. *Tel:* 413/586-6365. *Prop:* Barbara L. Feret.

Specializing in rare and op books on cooking, gastronomy, foodstuffs, and the literature of wine, the shop's stock numbers approximately 3000 volumes. Shop's business is conducted by mail order and by appointment.

Marblehead

'NEATH THE ELMS. 295 Washington St., Marblehead, MA 01945. *Tel:* 617/631-6222. *Proprs:* Bob and Lorraine Allison. *Hours:* Open all year, daily 10 to 6:00.

A small, well chosen general collection. Specialties are New England and nautical books, including handsome and still useful sea charts. Some very fine old maps are available.

Take the Salem exit off Rte. 128, then Rte. 114 to Marblehead. The shop is near the town hall.

Mashpee

CAPE COD BOOK CENTER. Rte. 28, Mashpee, MA. *Tel:* 617/477-9903. *Prop:* Carole W. Aronson. *Hours:* Open all year, seven days a week 10 to 6:00.

This shop advertises "We make it fun to browse," but the staff is not intrusively affable. It is a comfortable place and the general stock of thousands of books in all subject areas, hard and soft cover, permits some serious browsing. Customers are offered a cup of coffee and though the proprietor might be too amiable to do more than suggest that you drink it away from the books, I do not hesitate to forbid it. (Do not drink beverages or consume foods, or smoke, or permit your children to approach books while eating candy or chewing gum. They should not be chewing gum, in any case, in a bookshop.)

The shop is located on the Barnstable/Mashpee line.

Newton

THE BOOK COLLECTOR. 375 Elliot St., Newton, MA 02164. *Tel:* 617/964-3599. *Prop:* Ted Berman. *Hours:* Open all year, Monday thru Saturday 10 to 5:00.

A stock of 30,000 well chosen, rare, used and out of print books are found here. It is heartening to see bookshops like the Book Collector in the suburbs. The young suburban reader/collector may not realize that a bookstore, traditionally, is not a hole in the wall in a mall, crammed with best sellers and staffed by pleasant enough, but sometimes book-ignorant cashiers.

From Rte. 128 (I-95), take Rte. 9 toward Boston, take first exit on right (Chestnut St.), then first right (Ellis St.), first right again (Chestnut St. again), then first right at traffic light (Elliot St.).

Oak Bluffs

BOOK DEN EAST. New York Ave., PO Box 721, Oak Bluffs, MA 02557. *Tel:* 617/693-3946. *Proprs:* Richard and Susan Phelps. *Hours:* June thru October 10 to 6:00 daily; November thru May by appointment.

Difficult to miss because of the paint-box bright flowers in tubs in the front yard.

The shop is in a turn-of-the-century barn adjacent to the house. A general stock of 18,000 thoughtfully selected books, in all subjects. This is another useful source for the home library builder. These books are in unusually fine condition. The collector will find excellent selections in this shop's respectable collections of juveniles, travel, literature and literary criticism, navigation and natural history.

Located on Martha's Vineyard Island, near the ferry landing on the road between Oak Bluffs and Vineyard Haven.

Palmer

FOX HILL BOOKS. 436 Main St., PO Box 523, Palmer, MA 01069. *Tel:* 413/283-7681. *Prop:* Richard C. Taylor. *Hours:* Open all year, Monday thru Saturday 9 to 5:00 or by appointment.

General stock of 5 to 7000 volumes with specialties in children's books, Indians and Americana. Good browsing.

The shop is located one mile from Exit 8 off Mass. Turnpike.

THE OPEN CREEL. 25 Breton St., PO Box 523, Palmer, MA 01069. *Tel:* 413/283-7681 or 283-3960. *Proprs:* Dick and Joan Taylor. *Hours:* By appointment only.

This bookshop has a small stock concentrating solely on titles about fishing. The shop is located two miles from Exit 8 off the Mass. Turnpike.

Pittsfield

IMAGINE THAT. 58 Dalton Ave., Pittsfield, MA 01201. *Tel:* 413/445-5934. *Hours:* Open all year, everday from 10 to 5:00.

A general stock shop of more than 20,000 used books, magazines, comics, gum cards, posters, very scarce old paperbacks and video items. Considering the reluctance of some booksellers to accept paper ephemera, such as posters and even paperbacks, as legitimate collector specialties, it will be interesting to watch the development of video material as a collection specialty.

Located one mile east of Main St. (Rte. 7).

SECOND FLOOR BOOKS. 47 North St., Pittsfield, MA 01201. *Tel:* 413/442-6876. *Prop:* Eric Wilska. *Hours:* Open all year, 10:30 to 4:30 daily.

A general interest shop in business since 1974, with approximately 25,000 volumes arranged by subject. This shop has a large collection of sensibly priced first editions and Berkshire County titles. Hal Borland is a specialty.

The shop is located in downtown Pittsfield, the Berkshire County seat. North St. is Rte. 7, the main north/south route thru the county.

Salem

SAXIFRAGE BOOKS. 13 Central St., Salem, MA 01970. *Tel:* 617/745-7170. *Proprs:* Gina Shulimson, Deborah Wender, Gerry Williams. *Hours:* Open all year, Tuesday thru Saturday 12 to 6:00.

This is not a general stock book store. There are exceptionally well chosen titles in natural history, art books, first editions and some of the nicest illustrated and children's books — Walter Crane, Rackham, Howard Pyle and others.

Deborah Wender is a professional bookbinder. Edition and special binding are also available on the premises.

The proprietors have earned an excellent reputation among dealers and reader/collectors.

Take Rte. 128 to Rte. 114 into Salem or 1A directly into Salem.

Southbridge

ROLAND BOUTWELL — BOOKS. 62 Elms St., Southbridge, MA 01550. *Tel:* 617/765-0370. *Hours:* By chance or appointment.

A general stock of several thousand books in subjects from art to zoology.

South Egremont

BOOKS IN THE BERKSHIRES. Rte. 23, PO Box 404, South Egremont, MA 01258. *Tel:* 413/528-2327 — shop, 413/528-9499 — home. *Proprs:* Bruce and Susan Guenter. *Hours:* Open Memorial Day to Thanksgiving everyday, except Tuesday, from 10:30 to 5:00; rest of year, open Friday, Saturday and Sunday from 10:30 to 5:00; also by appointment.

Shop has a large general stock of biography, history, fiction and art, remainders and publishers' closeouts.

The shop specializes in 19th century women's fashion magazines, with hand-colored plates. This specialty is being expanded to other types of periodicals and books with hand colored plates, and prints.

Located in town on Rte. 23.

South Hamilton

ELMCRESS BOOKS. 161 Bay Rd., Rte. 1A, South Hamilton, MA 01982. *Tel:* 617/468-3261. *Proprs:* Britta and Cheever Cressy. *Hours:* Open all year, Tuesday thru Saturday noon to 5:00.

Located in the center of Hamilton at the railroad crossing, 3 miles north of Rte. 128 on Rte. 1A, Elmcress has a general stock of books, plus specialties, ships and the sea, and books on books.

South Lee

J & J LUBRANO. PO Box 47, South Lee, MA 01260. *Tel:* 413/243-2218. *Proprs:* John and Jude Lubrano.

The Lubranos specialize in performing arts titles: music, dance, theater, magic. With over 5000 rare and out of print volumes, this shop is an excellent source for materials in an enchanting specialty.

The depth and breadth of their collections reflects the proprietors' knowledge and discernment in a specialty that is not crowded. The shop also carries prints and autographs in the performing arts area.

Business is conducted by mail and by appointment.

Springfield

JOHNSON'S BOOKSTORE. 1379 Main St., Springfield, MA 01103. *Tel:* 413/732-6222. *Proprs:* The Johnson Family. *Hours:* Open all year, Monday thru Saturday 9 to 5:30, Thursday until 9:00.

Large general stock covering a wide range of subjects. Johnson's has a solid selection of remainder titles. Because many newly published books have a short shelf life, it is essential for the true reader/collector to know where a good stock of remainders can be found. The collector knows that the books that will be sought after in the future are not usually on today's best seller list.

Johnson's is located on Main and Market in front of Parking garage. Take Springfield Center exit off 91, first left at end of exit ramp, then first right onto Court St. — go straight thru intersection of Main and Court Sts. for parking.

West Bridgewater

THE BOOKSTORE OF WEST BRIDGEWATER. 222 North Main St., West Bridgeport, MA 02379. *Hours:* Open all year, Saturday and Sunday from 12 to 6:00.

A general stock of 50,000 used, rare and out-of-print books.

West Brookfield

THE BOOK BEAR. Rte. 9 — Box 663, West Brookfield, MA 01585. *Tel:* 617/867-8705. *Prop:* Albert Navitski. *Hours:* Open all year, Wednesday thru Sunday 10 to 6:00; other times by appointment or chance.

As a Harvard student, Thomas Wolfe (*Look Homeward Angel*) supposedly dashed up and down the aisles of the Widener Library half mad with the realization that one lifetime was too short to read all the books on the Widener shelves.

The proprietor of the Book Bear has a more pragmatic, though no less romantic view of this eternal dilemma.

"I like to think that you absorb books through your fingers, through the dust. Just being in the presence of books is enjoyable. It both dwarfs and astounds people — like John Muir's writing about nature — the sheer number of books in the world. I enjoy knowing they're there, even though I know I can't ever encompass them."

The Book Bear is in the Navitski's home, a large, white house of many rooms. "30,000 books looking for good homes" is not merely an advertisement for the shop, but the statement of a personal mission. "We delight in matching book to customer."

Specialties in psychology and the occult, and a general stock in a wide range of subjects, fiction and non-fiction.

Book Bear is on Rte. 9, 12 miles from old Sturbridge Village, and the Mass. Pike I-86 interchange, via Rte. 148.

West Concord

BOOKS WITH A PAST. 113 Commonwealth Ave., West Concord, MA 01742. *Tel:* 617/371-0180. *Proprs:* Susan Tucker and Anne Wanzer. *Hours:* Open all year, Monday thru Saturday 10 to 5:00.

A general stock of "goodies, cheapies, rare and out of print books." Shop's specialties include Concord area history, transcendentalism, and books by and about Concord authors.

Shop is ½ mile from the Rte. 2 rotary.

West Stockbridge

DOROTHY ELSBERG. Box 178, West Stockbridge, MA 01266. *Tel:* 413/232-8560. *Prop:* Dorothy Elsberg. *Hours:* By appointment.

Specializing in musical literature, rare and out of print books and sheet music, this shop's business is conducted by mail or appointment. Musical literature is a demanding and to the musically illiterate, an arcane, specialty in the trade. For the

163

expert it can be more than spiritually rewarding — Debussy's manuscript for his opera *Pelleas et Melisande* brought $350,000 at Christies New York Book Department auction on May 21, 1982. The price set a new world's record for a musical manuscript.

Williamstown

THE OLD BOOK SHOP at the Carriage Barn on Combined Rtes. 2 and 7, PO Box 366, Williamstown, MA 01267. *Tel:* 413/458-5534 — Home, 413/458-9326 — Barn. *Prop:* Martha Mercer. *Hours:* May 1 to December 1, Monday thru Saturday 10 to 5:00, Sunday 12 to 5:00; other times by appointment at the home number.

The proprietor of the Old Book Shop usually extends her welcome on an oversized calling card so why not here?

"A warm, congenial atmosphere welcomes you to browse through the clean, well-lighted collection of 20,000 scholarly and collectible books." Limited editions, travel, exploration, New Englandiana, Women, Medicine, poetry, fine arts, the Occult, theater, children's books are only a partial list of the well chosen stock.

The shop is housed in the red carriage barn built for summer resident John Wanamaker's carriages one hundred years ago.

Located two miles south of Williams Inn and situated next to the Elwal Pines Motel and the LeJardin Restaurant.

Worcester

ISAIAH THOMAS BOOKS AND PRINTS. 980 Main St., Worcester, MA 01603. *Tel:* 617/750-0750. *Prop:* Jim Visbeck. *Hours:* Open all year; Tuesday, Thursday and Friday 12 to 5:00; Wednesday 12 to 9:00; Saturday 9 to 5:00 and by appointment; Sunday 12 to 5:00 (except May to August).

Named for America's most famous printer-journalist, Isaiah Thomas (1749-1831), this shop specializes in first editions, original prints and reproductions. There is also a carefully selected general stock.

Yarmouth Port

PARNASSUS BOOK SERVICE. Rte. 6A, Yarmouth Port, MA 02675. *Tel:* 617/362-6420. *Proprs:* Ben and Ruth Muse. *Hours:* June to August, Monday thru Saturday 9 to 9:00, Sunday 12 to 5:00; September to May, Monday thru Saturday 9 to 5:30.

Shop is in a landmark (1840) three story, clapboarded New Englander, originally a general store. A good stock of 100,000 books arranged by categories in room after tidy room makes the Parnassus another browser's paradise.

Fine out-of-print books on antiques and crafts, both American and foreign, are a specialty of the shop. Other specialties are New Englandia, maritime titles, including not easily obtainable Caribbean watershed titles, and a solid selection in ornithology.

New Hampshire

Bradford

KALONBOOKS. Rte. 114, Box 16, Bradford, NH 03221. *Tel:* 603/938-2380. *Prop:* Rod Jones. *Hours:* Saturday and Sunday 1 to 5:00; daily in July and August.

This shop specializes in American history, biography, literature, first editions, criticism and a small selection of science fiction. Also general titles.

The shop will be carrying University Press remainders on American history. More bookshops should carry University Press books in subject areas suitable to their specialties. These books are difficult to get though many University Press titles are of interest to the reader/collector.

The University of Nebraska Press has published Willa Cather's previously un-collected short stories, and her very early articles and reviews; few retail bookshops would consider carrying these books and it is unlikely that the chain shops could find space amidst their exercise and cookery and mass market titles.

Kalonbooks is located ¼ mile north of Rtes. 103 and 114 junction at the blinking light.

Center Sandwich

THE ELL SHOP. Rte. 113, Center Sandwich, NH 03227. *Tel:* 603/284-6256. *Prop:* Clara W. Roth. *Hours:* Open June thru October, daily 9 to 5:00.

Besides a general stock of about 5000 books, this shop carries prints and posters.
The shop is located a mile west of the village on Rte. 113.

Contoocook

EMERY'S BOOKS. Rte. 2, Duston Rd., Contoocook, NH 03229. *Tel:* 603/746-4474. *Prop:* Ron and Charlotte Emery. *Hours:* Open by chance or appointment.

Emery's publishes 10 to 15 catalogues a year, titles in all categories but subjects occuring most frequently are travel and exploration, Americana, natural history, science and medicine, maps and journals.

Emery's offers a book auction by mail — most books sell for $5 to $30. The cost of 5 catalogues with prices realized is $10.

All books from the regular catalogues are returnable if not satisfactory. This is true of almost all catalogue sales. Auction purchases are returnable at Emery's for just cause, although this is rarely if ever done at other auctions.

Duston Rd. is off Rte. 202 between Hopkinton and Henniker.

WOMEN'S WORDS BOOKS. 12 Main St., Box 295, Contoocook, NH 03229. *Tel:* 603/746-4483. *Proprs:* Ann Grossman, Nancy Needham. *Hours:* Open all year, Tuesday thru Saturday 10 to 5:00, Sunday 1 to 5:00. Search Service Mail Order.

This may be the only shop in New England established primarily to preserve and promote the reading and collecting of women's history, biography, poetry and fiction. There is a general stock of over 15,000 books with a large and varied selection of books by and about women. There are well chosen titles and authors: Aphra Ben, Louisa May Alcott, George Eliot, Kay Boyle, Louise Bogan, Betty Friedan, the Brontes, Mrs. Trollope, Mary Austin and Jane Austen, and others. Nineteenth century and earlier books on the training and education of women (usually written by men) and "female hygiene" books (always written by men) should be read by anyone, male or female, who has ever wondered what intellectual dyspepsia on the subject of women influenced Freud to become such a disagreeable little nuisance.

The shop is located on Main St. (Rte. 103) just about in the center of town.

Dublin

THE BOOKCASE. Rte. 101, Box 96, Dublin, NH 03444. *Tel:* 603/547-3354. *Prop:* Vivian Walsh. *Hours:* Please call ahead.

The Bookcase has a general stock of 15 to 20,000 volumes on all subjects.

Located one mile south of Greenfield Village with a book sign on lawn.

Gilford

LOUISE FRAZIER — BOOKS. Morrill St., Gilford, NH 03246. Mailing address: RFD 6, Box 477, Laconia, NH 03246. *Tel:* 603/524-2427. *Prop:* Louise Frazier. *Hours:* By chance or appointment.

General stock of 20,000 volumes with emphasis on biography and fiction.

Located on Rte. 11A out of Laconia toward Gilford. Morrill St. is third street on left, then about two miles to house. There is a sign on the lawn.

Henniker

BOOK FARM. Concord Rd., Henniker, NH 03242. *Tel:* 603/428-3429. *Prop:* Walter Robinson. *Hours:* September thru May, Saturday and Sunday 12 to 5:00; June thru August, daily 12 to 5:00.

General stock of 30,000 volumes with emphasis on modern firsts, literature, literary history and biography, New England, fine press books.

Located 15 miles west of Concord, New Hampshire, on Rtes. 202 and 9.

Hillsboro

THE SHADOW SHOP. Preston St., Box 942, Hillsboro, NH 03244. *Tel:* 603/464-5413. *Proprs:* Lois and Barbara Meredith. *Hours:* Open all year, Tuesday thru Saturday 10 to 5:00, Sunday and Monday by chance or appointment.

The shop has a general stock with specialties in advertising ephemera and post-cards. Advertising material is varied and nicely preserved. Some fine examples of 19th century trade cards.

Take exit 5 from I-89 to Rte. 202. Turn north off 202 at Reade and Woods Insurance Agency.

Hollis

STILE'S BARN. 108 Depot Rd., Hollis, NH 03049. *Tel:* 603/465-2543. *Proprs:* Arthur and Josephine Stiles. *Hours:* Open all year by chance or appointment.

This shop has a good number of western Indian, military, illustrated and cook books. There are fine natural history books from the 1700s on. The Barn also carries a large stock of prints and engravings, steel and wood.

The proprietors advise calling ahead.

Hollis is about 10 miles west of Nashua near the intersection of Rtes. 130 and 122.

Laconia

BARN LOFT BOOKSHOP. 96 Woodland Ave., Laconia, NH 03246. *Tel:* 603/524-4839. *Prop:* Lee
Burt. *Hours:* Please call ahead or by chance; closed January and February.

This shop specializes in children's books and New England; there is a general stock
of fiction and non-fiction, carefully selected.

From Laconia High School on Union Ave. going north toward Lakeport, take
first right (Lyman St.), next right (Butler St.) and left onto Woodland Ave.

Marlborough

HOMESTEAD BOOKSHOP. Rte. 101, Box 90, Marlborough, NH 03455. *Tel:* 603/876-4610.
Proprs: Harry and Connie Kenney. *Hours:* Summer, daily 8:30 to 5:00, Saturday and Sunday 9 to 4:30;
Winter, October 15 thru April 15, daily except Sunday 8:30 to 4:30.

The Homestead Bookshop has a general stock of 30,000 books, with a specialty in
children's books.

The shop is located on Main St. (Rte. 101) in town.

Meredith

MARY ROBERTSON BOOKS. Parade Rd. and Rte. 3, Box 296, Meredith, NH 03253. *Tel:*
603/279-8750 or 279-6015. *Prop:* Mary Robertson. *Hours:* Summer, daily 10 to 5:00; Spring and Fall,
weekends or by appointment.

This shop has a general stock in most subject areas.

North Weare Village

SYKES AND FLANDERS. Rte. 77, North Weare Village, NH 03281. *Tel:* 603/529-7432. *Proprs:*
Richard and Mary Sykes. *Hours:* Open all year by appointment or by chance.

Thoughtfully selected titles in natural history, illustrated books, detective fiction,
travel and exploration, first editions and Americana.

The shop is on Rte. 77 in the village, ½ mile from Rte. 114.

Ossipee

HODSDON FARM BOOKS. Baker's Peel at Sunny Villa, Rte. 16, Ossipee, NH 03864. *Tel:*
603/539-2252. *Proprs:* Gerard, Jr. and Christine Powers. *Hours:* All year, daily 9 to 5:00.

General stock with a good selection of New England, New Hampshire, Maine and
White Mountain titles, fiction and non-fiction.

Books are stocked at the Sunny Villa Restaurant and Baker's Peel next door all
year. The barn at Hodson Farm is open summers and by appointment.

Portsmouth

THE BOTTOM LINE. 68 State St., Portsmouth, NH 03801. *Tel:* 603/431-8376. *Prop:* Julie Fast.
Hours: Open all year, Monday thru Saturday 10 to 7:00, Friday 10 to 9:00, Sunday 12 to 5:00.

There is good browsing in this shop, with new and used books on alternative
living, solar and wood heat, organic gardening, herbs, building instruction books
and a general line of literature, including the classics.

Located around the corner from Strawberry Banke and Prescott Park.

Rumney

STINSON HOUSE. Quincy Rd., Rumney Village, Rumney, NH 03266. *Tel:* 603/786-3962 or 786-9898. *Proprs:* George and Anne Kent. *Hours:* Please call ahead or by chance.

A general stock of 30,000 volumes is housed in a large barn; in the house are Americana, New Hampshire and White Mountain titles.

Stinson House is in Rumney Village off Rte. 125, seven miles west of Plymouth, New Hampshire.

Wolfeboro

BOOKENDS BOOKSHOP. PO Box 1812, Lehner St., Wolfeboro, NH 03894. *Tel:* 603/569-5438. *Proprs:* JoEllen Scully, Robert Brokaw. *Hours:* Monday thru Saturday 10 to 6:00, Sunday 10 to 4:00.

A new shop and a fine one on all counts. The main shop has a good selection of fiction and non-fiction, and a children's section. Specialties in psychology, science, history are upstairs, sets too.

This is a reader's shop, bright and orderly, with the comfortable stir and quiet exhilaration present when real readers meet real books.

Bookends has a section of first editions, many signed, all in fine condition, none priced higher than a couple of dollars. "Dealers and collectors are welcome, of course, but our philosophy is that books should once again be affordable luxuries for readers," say the proprietors.

Bookends runs ads in local papers listing some of their books with prices. Most are under a dollar — even the remainder tables can't match these prices. I'd like to see more used book shops run these ads.

Shop is at the Dandelion Florist Shop, off Main St.

Rhode Island

Bristol

THE CURRENT COMPANY. 12 Howe St., Bristol, RI 02809. *Tel:* 401/253-7824. *Prop:* Robert R. Miller, ABAA. *Hours:* Open all year, Monday thru Friday 9 to 4:30, weekends by appointment.

Mr. Miller conducts a world-wide mail and telephone order business from a re-modeled carriage house containing 10,000 books, prints, autographed letters — signed, and related items.

Current Company specializes in Americana, American and English literature, Voyages and Travels, Marine (including one of the largest collections centered on American Cup racing), fine press books, and other subjects of interest to the collector.

Shop is located two blocks from Rte. 114. If you have difficulty finding it, Mr. Miller suggests that you call for detailed instructions.

Cranston

PATRICK T. CONLEY, BOOKS. 43 Windsor Rd., Cranston, RI 02905. *Tel:* 401/785-0169. *Hours:* Open all year, by appointment.

Mr. Conley carries about 5000 volumes in Americana, the American Civil War, Law, Literary Criticism, New England and Rhode Island, also Western Americana and titles on the American South.

Rhode Island seems to make up for its small geographical size by the complexity of its topography. Mr. Conley sends the following directions: Take Thurbers Ave. exit from I-95 in Providence to Allens Ave. Go south'(away from Providence center) on Allens Ave. for 2.2 miles (Allens becomes Narragansett Blvd. at Cranston city line) then go right on Windsor Rd.

Newport

CORNER BOOK SHOP. 418 Spring St., Newport, RI 02840. *Tel:* 401/846-8406. *Hours:* Open all year, Monday thru Saturday 1 to 5:00, 6:30 to 9:00.

This shop opened in 1962 and has a varied and interesting general stock, in addition to a small stock of rare and out of print Americana. General stock includes sets and bindings, literature, cookboos and gardening, state and local history, exploration books with plates and engravings, modern, illustrated books, first, signed, and limited editions, reasonably priced out-of-print books, and a well-chosen, large general stock.

Providence

IRON HORSE COMICS AND COLLECTIBLES. 834 Hope St., Providence, RI 02906. *Tel:* 401/521-9343. *Proprs:* Sam and Geraldine Galentree. *Hours:* Open all year, Monday thru Thursday 10 to 6:00, Friday and Saturday 10 to 8:00.

Over 50,000 new and back issue comic books from 1924 to the present. Iron Horse does a brisk mailorder business in addition to its shop trade.

Mr. Galentree draws a comic strip for a local newspaper, appropriately enough.

The shop sponsors bi-monthly comic book conventions in nearby Pawtucket. "Tons" of paper Americana are displayed by New England comic book dealers at these meetings, where original comic book art occasionally surfaces. Movie ephemera and vintage paperbacks are also available at these well organized events.

SEWARD'S FOLLY. 139 Brook St., Providence, RI 02906. *Tel:* 401/272-4454. *Proprs:* Schuyler and Peterkin Seward. *Hours:* All year, Wednesday thru Sunday 12 to 8:00, Saturday 9 to 8:00.

Although the shop has a small collection of first editions the Sewards remain faithful to the original purpose of the shop which, Mr. Seward states is, "not to sell first editions to dealers, but books to readers. You should be able to walk out of a bookstore with the feeling that you found exactly the book you wanted, at a fair price."

The shop has a general stock of 12,000 books with emphasis on the proprietors' own interest in philosophy, American history, nature, agriculture and a growing Lincoln collection.

The Sewards are also developing a collection in 19th century American reform movements.

Some fine classics in sets: Dickens, Conrad, Irving, Twain; there is a lot of depth and variety in this shop's sound fiction titles.

Shop is ten blocks south of Brown University.

TYSON'S OLD AND RARE BOOKS. 334 Westminster St., Providence, RI 02900. *Tel:* 401/421-3939. *Hours:* Winter, 10 to 4:00, Saturday 10 to 1:00, closed Wednesday and Sunday; Summer, 10 to 4:00, closed Saturday and Sunday.

Tyson's premises are on the second floor. The shop specializes in Americana,

Rhode Island titles, and first editions. From I-95, 5 minutes away in downtown Providence, next to Grace Church on the mall. From I-95 north, take the Broadway exit; from I-95 south, Atwells Ave. exit.

Warwick

FORTUNATE FINDS BOOKSHOP. 14 West Natick Rd., Warwick, RI 02886. *Tel:* 401/737-8160. *Hours:* Open all year, Friday and Saturday 9 to 5:00, and by appointment.

Specializing in children's books as well as trade cards and trade catalogues, the shop issues catalogues listing stock in these areas. There are approximately 20,000 general stock books.

For over twenty years, Fortunate Finds has been conducting a Labor Day Outdoor Sale, which starts on the Sunday before Labor Day and goes through the week to the following Sunday.

There is also a book auction once a year but no fixed date.

Watch Hill

BOOK AND TACKLE SHOP. 7 Bay Rd., Watch Hill, RI 02891. *Tel:* 401/596-0700. *Hours:* Open June 20 thru September 6, 7 days a week, 10 to 9:00.

Books wait for us in the most improbable places, but booklovers consider no place incongruous, rather, they respect the impulse that gives books safe harbor.

On the Bay Rd. in Watch Hill, the Book and Tackle Shop reminds us of two of man's most satisfying pursuits.

Outside the shop are racks of postcards. Inside, there are old and antique postcards and 50,000 rare, out-of-print, old and recent titles covering a wide range of subjects. Specialties are cookbooks, medicine, nature, travel, science, and, of course, the sea.

Watch Hill is situated between Little Narragansett Bay and Block Island Sound.

Vermont

Bennington

BRADFORD BOOKS. West Rd., Rte. 9, Bennington, VT 05201. *Tel:* 802/447-0387 or 442-6216. *Hours:* May thru November, Wednesday thru Saturday 11 to 5:00, Sunday 1 to 5:00, or by appointment.

Shop has a general stock of old and out of print books, and like most shops, provides a search service.

Located on West Rd. opposite Fairdale Farms.

Binghamville

EXCEPTIONAL BOOKS. Binghamville, VT 05444. *Tel:* 802/849-6910. *Hours:* May 15 thru October 15, Tuesday, Thursday and Saturday 10 to 4:00, or by appointment.

This is another delightful small shop. Well organized, orderly shelving encourages serious browsing.

Over 3000 high quality New England titles with an emphasis on Vermont fiction and non-fiction.

Shop is 5 miles from Fairfax Rte. 104; stay on hardtop. If you are coming from Cambridge on Rte. 15 take a sharp left at Fletcher Center.

Cavendish

PINEMEADOW BOOKSTORE. RFD 1, Box 49, Cavendish, VT 05142. *Tel:* 802/226-7266. *Hours:* Open May to November, 10 to 4:00.

The shop has a general stock of about 6000 volumes with special emphasis on New England local histories and Americana. Pinemeadow also carries a large and varied selection of antique postcards.

The pursuit of books is seldom more challenging than when it leads us into remote regions of rural New England. Two roads diverging in a wood might give a poet pause, but to the bookseeker they only add zest to the chase.

Take exit 6 from I-91. Take 103 to 131 to center of Cavendish; from the Post Office in Cavendish go one mile to Whitesville Rd.; take left onto Whitesville and continue across bridge where the road becomes Center Rd. to Davis Rd. (.7 mile) left on David Rd. for .2 mile to Pinemeadow Bookstore.

Craftsbury Common

CRAFTSBURY COMMON ANTIQUARIAN. Craftsbury Common, VT 05827. *Tel:* 802/586-9677. *Proprs:* Ralph and Nancy Lewis. *Hours:* Open May thru August and on weekends by appointment or chance.

The Antiquarian has a carefully selected general stock with specialty titles in maritime subjects and the illustrated book.

Take Hwy. 14 to Craftsbury Common. From the common, drive .4 mile to where paved road curves left. Drive straight onto the dirt road about 40 yards then take first right for .4 mile to a house surrounded by high cedars. Shop's sign is out front.

Cuttingsville

HAUNTED MANSION BOOKSHOP. Rte. 103, Cuttingsville, VT 05738. *Tel:* 802/492-3337. *Proprs:* Clint, Lucille and Gary Fiske. *Hours:* May thru November 15, daily 9 to 5:00; otherwise by appointment.

Housed in a Victorian mansion, a delight to architectural historians, this shop stocks about 60,000 volumes in a wide range of subjects. The large collections of Vermontiana and Americana include unusual titles, and the odd, privately printed memoir that sometimes brings the history of some small town more vividly to life than the town's official history.

Shop carries an interesting selection of old maps and prints.

Shop is 10 miles south of Rutland on Rte. 103.

Fairfax

THE BOOKSTORE. Main St., Fairfax, VT 05454. *Proprs:* Arthur and Louise Wold. *Hours:* Open May thru October, Tuesday thru Friday 1 to 5:00, Saturday 10 to 4:00.

A pleasant shop in an unspoiled, northern Vermont town. The Bookstore has a general stock of used and out of print books that numbers in the thousands. It is always gratifying to see the wide variety of good used books available in rural shops like this.

Fairlee

THE OLD BOOK SHOP. Chapman's Pharmacy, Rte. 5, Fairlee, VT 05045. *Tel:* 802/333-9709. *Proprs:* John Larson and Odie Chapman.

The shop has a general browsing stock of about 5000 hardcover books, 15,000 collectible post cards and a large selection of paper ephemera. "If you don't see it, just ask for it!"

Located at Chapman's Pharmacy (prescriptions filled while you browse), about ½ mile from the Fairlee exit off I-91.

Lyndonville

GREEN MOUNTAIN BOOKS AND PRINTS. 100 Broad St., Lyndonville, VT 05851. *Tel:* 802/626-5051. *Proprs:* Ralph Secord, Jim and Ellen Doyle. *Hours:* All year, Monday thru Thursday 10 to 4:00, Saturday 10 to 1:00.

This is one of my favorite bookshops. It is large enough for serious browsing and there are unexpected recesses with shelves of books from floor to ceiling. General stock of about 50,000 books with a large selection of art, history, biography and fiction. Shop stocks an interesting collection of rare books and first editions and prints. Good remainders here, not non-books but sound titles, e.g., *Nabokov/Wilson Letters*.

Shop is on corner across from old Lyndonville depot.

Manchester

JOHNNY APPLESEED BOOKSHOP. Manchester, VT 05254. *Tel:* 802/362-2458. *Prop:* Frederic F. Taylor. *Hours:* Open all year, Monday thru Saturday 9:30 to 5:00, Saturday 10 to 4 or 5:00.

A venerable. In its fifty year history the shop has been patronized by American writers including Robert Frost, Carl Sandburg, Pearl Buck, America's first Nobel Laureate in Literature, Sinclair Lewis, and many others. Shop specialties are Vermont, American history, Americana, hunting and fishing, American first editions.

Located in an 1832 bank building on Rte. 7 in Manchester Village, next to the Equinox House.

Manchester Center

FIFE AND DRUM BOOKS. Rte. 1130, Manchester Center, VT 05255. *Proprs:* Bill and Elissa Eikner. *Hours:* Open all year from 10 to 5:00.

The specialties in the 5000 volumes here are American military history, political biography, and books on Vermont.

Located ½ block east of intersection of Rtes. 7 and 11-30.

KNEE DEEP IN BOOKS. Elm St., Manchester Center, VT 05255. *Tel:* 802/362-3663 or 867-4495. *Prop:* Pat Estey. *Hours:* Open April thru October, Tuesday thru Saturday 11 to 4:00; otherwise by chance or appointment.

The shop is in a blue barn with a cupola and has more than 10,000 books, general stock with a very good collection of books on fishing. They also do bookbinding. The shop is just off Rtes. 11-30, corner Center Hill Rd. and Elm St.

Middlebury

POOR RICHARD'S USED BOOK SHOP. 56 Main St., Middlebury, VT 05753. *Tel:* 802/388-3241. *Prop:* Lois Bestor Craig. *Hours:* Open April thru January, noon to 5:00.

The shop is a new venture for the owner whose family legacy of books could stock more than one shop. The 10,000 volumes selected for Poor Richard's consists of general stock with a wide range of titles.

Shop is located by the bridge.

THE VERMONT BOOK SHOP. 38 Main St., Middlebury, VT 05753. *Tel:* 802/388-2061. *Prop:* Robert Dike Blair. *Hours:* All year, Monday thru Saturday 9 to 5:00.

Shop carries out of print Vermont and New England titles.

Shop is in the middle of downtown.

Morrisville - Morristown Corners

BRICK HOUSE BOOK SHOP. Morristown Corners, Morrisville, VT 05661. *Tel:* 802/888-4300. *Prop:* Alexandra Heller. *Hours:* Open all year, daily except Mondays.

The shop is housed in two ground floor rooms of a local landmark, a large, square brick house, circa 1800. The stock is general, both hardcover and paperback, and numbers about 2000.

Shop is 2 miles south of Morrisville on Rte. 100, seven miles north of Stowe on Rte. 100.

Newport

MICHAEL DUNN, BOOKS. PO Box 436, Newport, VT 05855. *Tel:* 802/334-2768. *Prop:* Michael Dunn. *Hours:* Open all year by appointment.

Mr. Dunn's shop is located on Rte. 2, Eagle Point, Town of Derby, on the Canadian border. He specializes in titles about Vermont and Canada, as well as Americana, hunting, and fishing.

Plainfield

THE COUNTRY BOOKSHOP. Plainfield, VT 05667. *Tel:* 802/454-8439. *Proprs:* Benjamin and Alexandra Koenig. *Hours:* Open all year, Wednesday thru Saturday 10 to 5:00.

Folklore and books on bells are specialties in the stock here of about 10,000 books. There is also an interesting selection of postcards, prints and other paper ephemera.

Take Rte. 2 to Plainfield, turn at blinking light, then take the church driveway to the shop.

Putney

LILAC HEDGE BOOKSHOP. Westminster West Rd., Putney, VT 05346. *Tel:* 802/387-4445. *Proprs:* Katherine and Robert Ericson. *Hours:* All year, Thursday thru Sunday 10 to 5:00.

When we dream of the country bookshop we mean to open someday, we are dreaming of many bookshops, and Lilac Hedge is one of them, maybe *the* one. Serious browsers can settle down in the comfortable chairs near the polished woodstove in cool weather, or in lawn chairs outside under shade trees in warm weather.

About 8000 carefully selected books in all subjects with a respectable selection of art and children's books, and a growing collection of modern firsts.

Shop is about ¼ mile up Westminster West Rd. from the Putney General Store. Shop on left side of road. It is just a few minutes from exit 4 off I-91.

Rutland

TUTTLE ANTIQUARIAN BOOKS, INC. 28 South Main St., Rte. 7, Rutland, VT 05701. *Tel:* 802/773-8930 or 773-8229. *Prop:* Charles E. Tuttle. *Hours:* Open all year, Monday thru Friday 8 to 5:00.

A venerable. Book people love this shop. Like the green hills of Vermont, Tuttle's stands as a surety in an uncertain world. When we are away from Vermont, and things seem to be going like the last lines of "Dover Beach," we escape in our minds to Tuttle's pleasant, well-lighted browsing rooms, an agreeable switch from the "darkling plain."

The open stock of 20,000 volumes is well-chosen, and ranges across almost 50 subjects. Tuttle's specialties, genealogies, town and country histories and related material, are not in open stock, but are listed in catalogues for mail order customers.

Woodstock

ALLEGORY BOOK SHOP. 20 Central St., Woodstock, VT 05091. *Tel:* 802/457-3023. *Prop:* Bruce Hartman. *Hours:* Open all year, Tuesday thru Saturday, noon to 5:00, or by appointment.

Specializing in music, literature, history, the Allegory stocks about 3000 books in the shop which is located upstairs in the Morgan Block building just west of the Woodstock Post Office.

Take exit 2 off I-89, west about 10 miles to Woodstock, or take Rte. 4 west from White River Junction for about 15 miles.

Addenda to Used Book Sellers

Connecticut

Falls Village

THE OLD CHURCH. Main St., Falls Village, CT 06031. *Tel:* 203/824-0442. *Proprs:* R. and D. Emerson. *Hours:* By appointment only.

Fine books in all fields are included. The proprietors say "sorry, no children."

Maine

Freeport

MAVERICK BOOKS. Red Wheel Flea Market, Rte. 1, Freeport, ME in the summer and 79 Lincoln St., Portland, ME 04103 during the winter. *Tel:* 207/775-3233. *Prop:* Pat Murphy. *Hours:* In the summer, from 8 to 5:00 on Sundays only.

From May thru September, Maverick Books operates in Freeport; by mail order or phone during the rest of the year in Portland. The shop deals in rare, out of print and used books, with about 4000 volumes on display. The specialty is general non-fiction.

New Hampshire

Northwood

THE 1784 SHOP. Rte. 4, Box 550, Northwood, NH 03261. *Tel:* 603/942-8583. *Prop:* Richard G. Puffer. *Hours:* By chance or appointment.

A general stock of 10,000 volumes, with emphasis on New England titles is carried here. The shop also has prints and ephemera.
Located on Rte. 4 in Northwood Ridge.

Westmoreland

HURLEY BOOKS. Rte. 12, Westmoreland, NH 03467. *Tel:* 603/399-4342. *Prop:* Henry Hurley. *Hours:* Open all year by appointment or by chance.

There are about 20,000 books in this shop, and catalogs are issued regularly in religious history, Catholica (mainly 20th century, as Celtic Cross Books), farming and related materials. Miniature books are also available.
Located on Rte. 12, 200 yards north of Rte. 63.

Rhode Island

SIGN OF THE UNICORN. PO Box 297, Rte. 108, Peacedale, RI 02883. *Tel:* 401/789-8912. *Proprs:* Mary Jo Munroe, M.L.S., John Romano, Bookbinder. *Hours:* Open all year, Wednesday thru Saturday from 10 to 5:00.

Beginners are "more than welcome." Customers include students, faculty, and staff from nearby University of Rhode Island, "ardent collectors and kids from the adjacent playground with 25 cents to spend for a 'real book.' "

With another partner, Ms. Munroe conducts a mail order business centered on the very collectible paperback crime and detective fiction originals from the thirties to the present.

The general stock covers a wide range of interests: literature, feminism, very old American almanacs, one dated 1783, and more. Philosophy is presently quite popular at the Unicorn.

This is an ideal shop for the beginning collector and the home library builder, for here you can see the variety of humanity that is drawn to books, from the college professor seeking an out of print book for his research work, to the motorcyclist carefully fitting a just purchased set of Balzac into his saddlebags.

Sign of the Unicorn is at the rear of the Post Office in Peace Dale Center, appropriately, across from the Library. Off Rte. 1 in Wakefield, one mile from Wakefield on Rte. 108 heading toward University of Rhode Island in Kingston.

General Index

AB Bookman's Weekly, 63
American Book Collector Magazine, 63
American Book Prices Current, 53
Andersen, Hans Christian, 17
Armstrong, Margaret, 62
Azarian, Mary, 17
Baldwin, James, 79
Bay Psalm Book, 31, 52
Bennett, Arnold, 8
Bewick, Thomas, 17
Bowker, R.R., Company, 63
Bonn, Thomas L., 62
Breen, Jon L., 43
Brick Row, 131
Brooks, Van Wyck, 67
Carter, John, 61
Cather, Willa, 54-56
Collins, Benjamin, 17
Collins, Wilkie, 38
Corn Hill, 131
Crane, Walter, 13
Dahl, Roald, 18, 74
DaVinci, Leonardo, 7
De Brunhoff, Jean, 75
Dessauer, John P., 127
Doyle, Arthur Conan, 38
Enright, Elizabeth, 14
Ephemera Society of America, 25
Espey, John, 61-62
Folmsbee, Beulah, 14
Francis, Dick, 42
Gale Research Company, 53
Goody Two Shoes, 17
Gould, Stephen Jay, 79
Goytisolo, Juan, 66
Green, Hugh, 37
Grimm, Jacob and Wilhelm, 17
Gullans, Charles, 61-62
Hailey, Alex, 83
Hammer, Armand, 7
Hammett, Dashiell, 39
Hazard, Paul, 14, 79
Hoban, Russell, 130
Hoffman-Donner, Henrich, 15
Horn Book, Inc., 15
Howard, Peter B., 46, 62-63
Howes, Wright, 36, 48
Kemble, E. W., 51
King, Martin Luther, 7
Knopf, Alfred, 55
Leab, Daniel, 62
LeCarre, John, 42
Library of America, 67
Lorenz, Tom, 66
Melville, Herman, 8
Miller, Bertha Mahony, 15

Modern Language Assoc. (MLA), 68-69
Montessori, Maria, 78, 79
Muir, Percy, 63
Nabokov, Vladimir, 66
Neitz, John A., 19
Newbery, John, 17
Oriand, Michael V., 59-60
Orwell, George, 39
Panin, Dmitri, 46
Peters, Jean, 46, 61
Phippen, Sanford, 71
Poe, Edgar A., 37, 38
Power, Eileen, 23
Pushcart Prize, 72
Rackham, Arthur, 13
Readers, Heath and National, 75, 78
Rodriquez, Richard, 79
Rosenbach, A. S. W., 14
Sadleir, Michael, 8
Schatzki, Walter, 47
Sendak, Maurice, 74
Slung, Michele, 43
Solzhenitsyn, Alexander, 46
Stone, Wilbur Macey, 19
Suess, Dr., 74-75
Tanselle, G. Thomas, 62
Time Magazine, 8
Tracy, Jack, 43
Wertham, Frederick, 129
Wilson, Edmund, 68
Winks, Robin, 43

Index to Used Book Sales

Connecticut

Booth and Dimock Library (Coventry), 91
Cheshire Library, 91
Booth Library (Newtown), 93
Danbury Library, 91
Darien Library, 91
Groton Library, 92
Kent Library (Suffield), 95
Ladies Benevolent Society (Old Lyme), 94
The Ledyard Libraries, 92
Mystic and Noank Library, 92
New Haven Colony Historical Society, 93
Noyes Library (Old Lyme), 94
Oxford Library, 94
Pequot Library (Southport), 95
Sherman Library, 95

Smith College Club (New Canaan), 93
Stratford Library Association, 95
Twain Library (Redding), 94
Village Library (Farmington), 92
Wilton Library Association, 95

Maine

Boothbay Harbor Library, 96
Bristol Area Library, 97
Camden Library, 97
Casco Library, 97
Chase Emerson Library (Deer Isle), 98
Graves Library (Kennebunkport), 98
Jesup Library (Bar Harbor), 96
Jackson Library (St. George/Tenant's Harbor), 100
Libby Library (Old Orchard Beach), 99
North Bridgton Library, 99
North Haven Library, 99
Patten Free Library (Bath), 96
Prince Library (Cumberland Center), 98
Rangeley Library, 99
Rockland Library, 100
Rockport Library, 100
Skidompha Library (Damariscotta), 98
Skowhegan Library, 100
South Portland Armory, 101
Southport/Newagen Library, 101
Southwest Harbor Library, 101
Stonington Library, 101
Totman Library (Phippsburg), 99
Witherie Library (Castine), 98

Massachusetts

Acton Library, 102
Adams Library (Chelmsford), 104
Auburn Library, 102
Bellingham Library, 102
Belmont Library, 102, 103
Berkshire Athenaeum (Pittsfield), 107
Beverly Library, 103
Boxford Library, 103
Brandeis University Sale, 103
Buckingham, Browne and Nichols, 103-04
Cambridge Library, 103
Carnegie Library (Rockport), 108
Cary Library (Lexington), 106
Chilmark Library, 104
Concord Library, 105
Dartmouth Library, 108
Edgartown Library, 105
Eldredge Library (Chatham), 104

Fitchburg Library, 105
Friends Meeting House (Westport), 109
Hingham Library, 105
Hudson Library, 106
Hyde Library (Sturbridge), 108
Lincoln Library, 106
Lowell City Library, 106
Lynnfield Library, 106
Medford Library, 106
Morse Institute Library (Natick), 107
New Bedford Library, 107
Newton Free Library, 107
Sawyer Library (Gloucester), 106
Scituate Library, 108
Swampscott Library, 108
Waltham Library, 108
Wellesley Library, 109
Wenham Library, 109
Westborough Library, 109
West Falmouth Library, 109

New Hampshire

Amherst Library, 110
Bixby Memorial Library (Francestown), 112
Conway Library, 111
Derry Library, 111
Dublin Library, 111
Dimond Library, UNH, Durham, 112
Elins Library (Canterbury), 110
Five College Sale (Hanover), 112
Frost Library (Marlborough), 113
Gafney Library (Sanbornville), 115
Hookset Library, 113
Hopkinton Village Library, 113
Howe Library (Hanover), 113
Huggins Hospital Sale (Wolfeboro), 116
Kimball Library (Atkinson), 111
Lane Library (Hampton), 112
Littleton Library, 113
Meredith Library, 114
Moultonboro Library, 114
North Conway Library, 114
Foss Library (Center Barnstead), 110-11
Peterborough Library, 115
Richard Library (Newport), 114
Rochester Library, 115
Stowell Library (Cornish Flat), 111
Wolfeboro Library, 116

Rhode Island

Cross Mills Library (Charlestown), 117
Dodge Library (Block Island), 117
Hall Library (Cranston), 117
Harmony Library (Gloucester), 117
Lincoln Library, 118
Newport Library, 118
North Scitutate Library, 118
Providence Library, 118
Warwick Library, 118
Westerly Library, 118-19

Vermont

AAUW Sale (Brattleboro), 121-22
Aldrich Library (Barre), 121
Bennington Library, 121
Brandon Library, 121
Brooks Library (Brattleboro), 121
Brown Library (Northfield), 123
Brownell Library (Essex Junction), 122
Canfield Library (Arlington), 120-21
Chester Review Club (Chester Depot),
   122
Community Library (S. Burlington),
   125-26
Cutler Library (Plainfield), 123
Kellogg-Hubbard Library
   (Montpelier), 123
Lawrence Library (Bristol), 122
Pierson Library (Shelburne), 125
Poultney Library, 124
Morristown Library (Morrisville), 123
Peacham Library, 123-24
Proctor Library, 124
Quechee Library Association, 124
Reading Library, 125
Rutland Library, 125
St. Johnsbury Athenaeum, 125
Sherburne Library (Killington), 122
Skinner Library (Manchester), 122
Williams Library (Woodstock), 126
Windsor Library, 126
Winooski Library, 126
Wright Library (Pownal), 124

Index to Used Booksellers

Connecticut

Anglers' and Shooters' Bookshelf,
   137-38
Benson, Deborah, 140-41
Bibliolatree, 138
Book Block, The, 136
Bookie, The, 137
Branford Rare Books and Art Gallery,
   135
Bryn Mawr Book Shop, 138-39
Colebrook Book Barn, 136
Coventry Book Shop, 136
Farnsworth, Barbara, 140
Fine Literary Property, 139
Museum Gallery Book Shop, The, 137
Nutmeg Books, 140
Pages of Yesteryear, The, 139
Reese, William, Company, 138
Salk, Gil, Books and Birds, 136
Skutel, John, Galleries, 137
Whitlock Farm Booksellers, 135
Whitlock's Incorporated, 139

Maine

Anna's Books, 148
Bethel Book Barn, 142-43
Book Addict, The, 147
Bookbarn, The, 148
Book Cellar, 145
Book Loft, 147
Book Pedlars, 144
Bridgton Book House, 143
Bunkhouse Books, 145
Canney, Robert, Rare Books, 142
Carriage House, 147
Charles, M., Books, 148
Doughty's Falls Old Bookshop, 146
Eastman, Harland, Books, 149
Edgecomb Book Barn, 146
Harding, Douglas N., Rare Books, 150
Isaacson, Deborah, 145
Jonesport Wood Company, Inc., 150-51
Ledlie, Patricia, 144
Lippincott, Bill, Books, 143
Lobster Lane Book Shop, 149-50
MacDonald's Military Memorabilia
   and Maine Mementoes, 144
Medical Book Service Company, 143
Mirkwood Books, 151
O'Brien, F. M., Antiquarian Bookseller,
   147

Ockett, Moll, Antiques, 144
Old Book Shop, The, 145
Owen, Maurice, Books, 145-46
Pro Libris, 142
Robinson, Charles, Rare Books, 146
Seams, Colby, Books, 142
Varney's Volumes, 148
Walfield-Thistle, Inc., 144
Ward's, Nellie, Bookbarn, 150
Winter Farm Books, 147
Wood, Frank, Books, 149

Massachusetts

Barrow Bookstore, The, 157-58
Book Bear, The, 163
Book Collector, The, 160
Book Den East, 160
Books in the Berkshires, 161
Bookstore of West Bridgewater,
  The, 162
Books with a Past, 163
Boston Book Annex, 154
Boutwell, Roland, Books, 161
Brattle Book Shop, 154
Bromer Booksellers, 155
Bryn Mawr Book Sale, 157
Cape Cod Book Center, 159
Cookery Bookery, The, 159
Dunham's Bookstore, 153
Elmcress Books, 162
Elsberg, Dorothy, 163-64
Fox Hill Books, 160
Goodspeed's Book Shop, 155-56
Grolier Book Shop, 157
Imagine That, 160-61
Irene's Book Shop, 158
Johnson's Bookstore, 162
J & J Lubrano, 162
McKenna, Jean S., Books, 154
Morrill, Edward, and Sons, Inc., 155
'Neath The Elms, 159
Old Book Shop at the Carriage Barn,
  The, 164
Open Creel, The, 160
Parnassus Book Service, 164
Payson Hall Bookshop, 153
Saxifrage Books, 161
Second Floor Books, 161
Second Life Books, 152
Starr Book Company, Inc., 156
Staten Hook Books, 159
Ten Pound Island Book Company, 158
Thomas, Isaiah, Books and Prints, 164
Valley Bookshop, 153

New Hampshire

Barn Loft Bookshop, 168
Bookcase, The, 166
Bookends Bookshop, 169
Book Farm, 167
Bottom Line, The, 168
Ell Shop, The 165
Emery's Books, 166
Frazier, Louise, Books, 167
Homestead Bookshop, 168
Hodsdon Farm Books, 168
Kalonbooks, 165
Robertson, Mary, Books, 168
Shadow Shop, The, 167
Stile's Barn, 167
Stinson House, 169
Sykes and Flanders, 168
Women's Words Books, 166

Rhode Island

Book and Tackle Shop, 172
Conley, Patrick T., Books, 170-71
Corner Book Shop, 171
Current Company, The, 170
Fortunate Finds Bookshop, 172
Iron Horse Comics and Collectibles, 171
Seward's Folly, 171
Tyson's Old and Rare Books, 171-72

Vermont

Allegory Book Shop, 178
Bookstore, The, 174
Bradford Books, 173
Brick House Book Shop, 176
Country Bookshop, The, 177
Craftsbury Common Antiquarian, 174
Dunn, Michael, Books, 177
Exceptional Books, 173
Fife and Drum Books, 176
Green Mountain Books and Prints, 175
Haunted Mansion Bookshop, 175
Johnny Appleseed Bookshop, 175
Knee Deep In Books, 176
Lilac Hedge Bookshop, 177
Old Book Shop, The, 175
Poor Richard's Used Book Shop, 176
Pinemeadow Bookstore, 174
Tuttle Antiquarian Books, Inc., 178
Vermont Book Shop, The, 176